Between Waves

AF595899

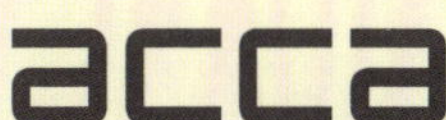

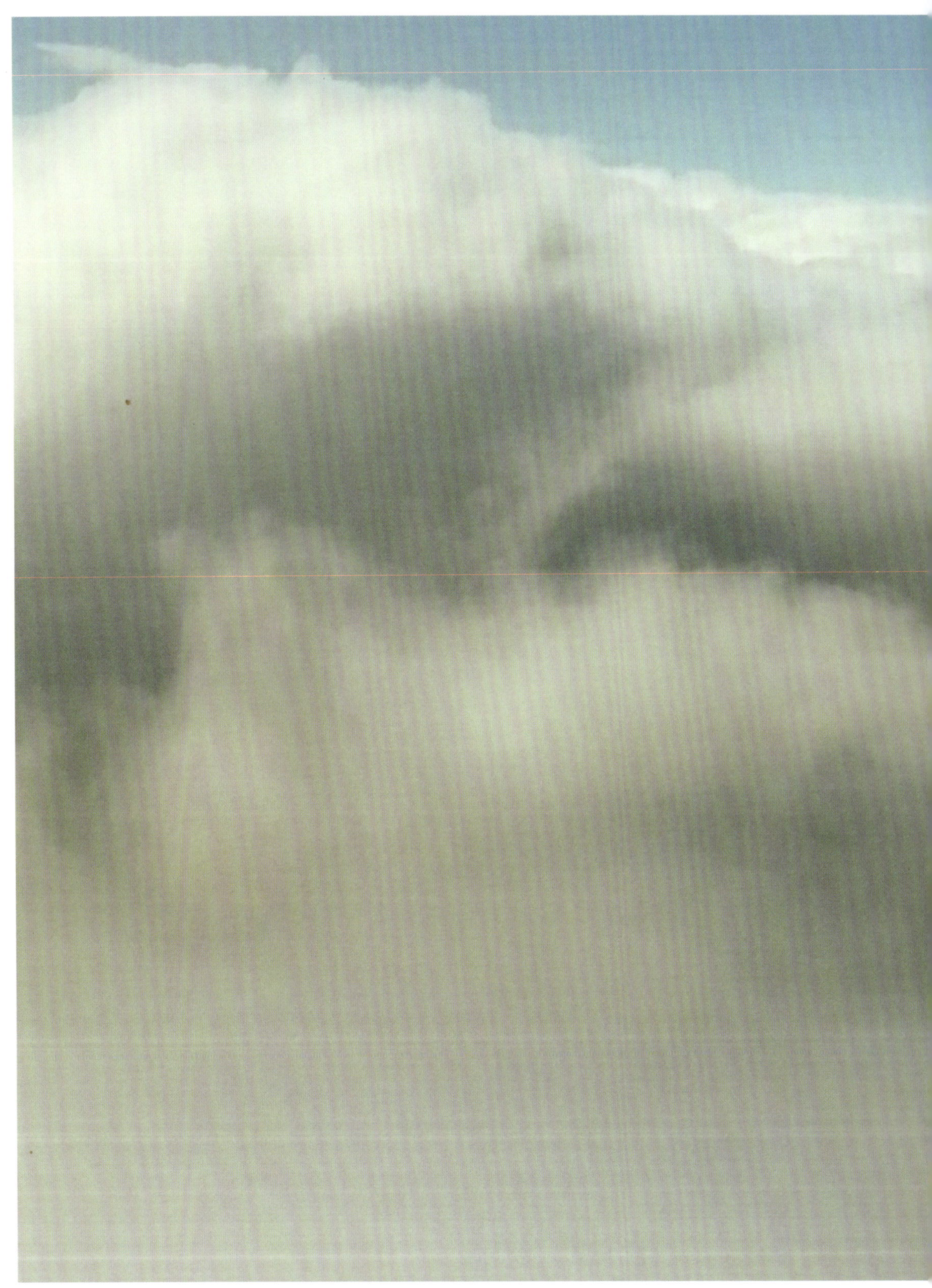

Jazz Money, *infinite iterative piece* 2023 (still)

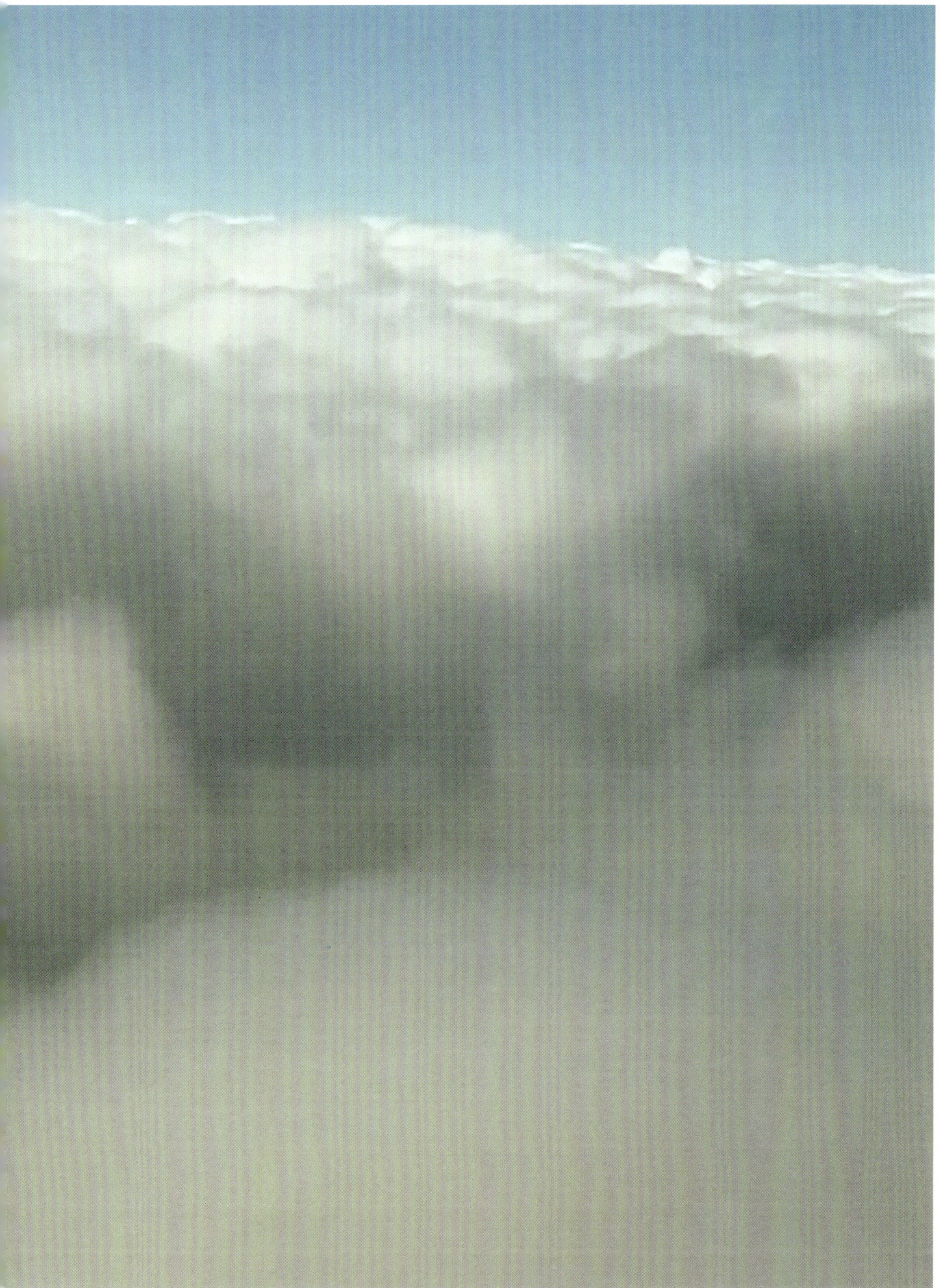

Advisory note: This publication references Aboriginal Ancestral remains and Aboriginal people who have passed.

Between Waves

Australian Centre For Contemporary Art
1 July – 3 September 2023

Maree Clarke
Dean Cross
Brad Darkson
Matthew Harris
James Howard
Hayley Millar Baker
Jazz Money
Cassie Sullivan
this mob
Mandy Quadrio

Curator: Jessica Clark

Contents

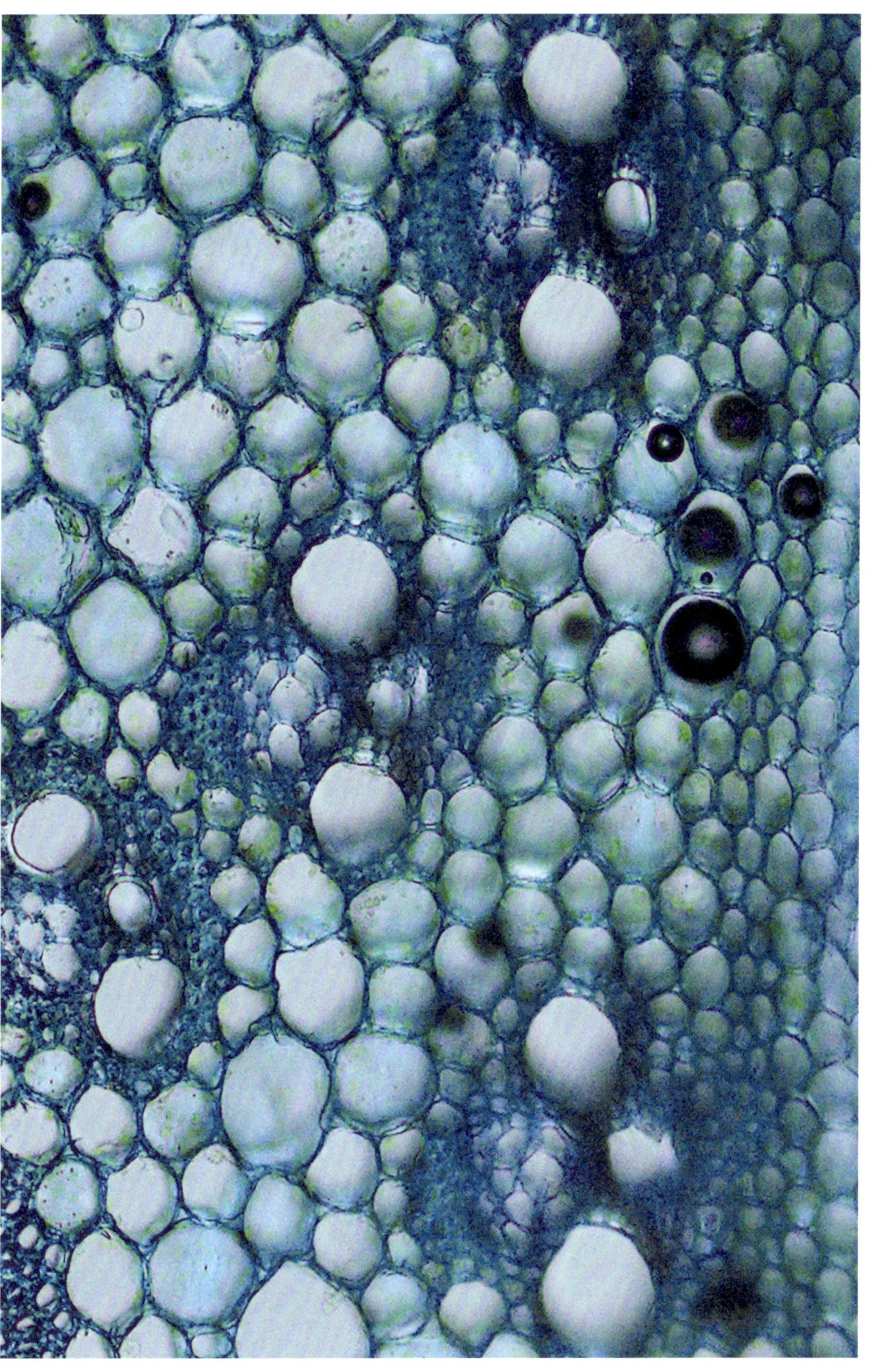

Maree Clarke, *now you see me: seeing the invisible #1* 2023 (detail)

Foreword

Navigating the intersections and collisions between art, culture, materiality and technologies, the Australian Centre for Contemporary Art is delighted to present *Between Waves*, which continues the Yalingwa exhibition series developed to support the development and highlight the significance of First Nations contemporary art and curatorial practice of the Southeast within a national context.

Between Waves amplifies concepts related to light, time and vision – and the idea of shining a light on our times – expressed by the Wurundjeri Woi Wurrung word 'Yalingwa'. The exhibition presents the work of ten artists and collectives who variously explore the visible and invisible energy fields set in motion by these ideas, to illuminate interconnected shapeshifting ecologies within, beyond and between what can be seen.

Established by Creative Victoria, in partnership with the Australian Centre for Contemporary Art and the TarraWarra Museum of Art, the Yalingwa initiative has been designed to provide a platform for First Nations artists and curators to develop their work within the context of a leading public art gallery and museum, as well as offering a substantial Fellowship for an artist who has made a significant contribution to contemporary First Nations art and cultural practice.

Between Waves has been curated by Jessica Clark who joined ACCA's staff in April 2022. It has been a great pleasure to work with Jess and to have her on the ACCA team, and to support her ambitious vision for the exhibition which has been undertaken with intelligence, deep thinking and care. I would like to equally extend our sincere thanks and appreciation to the participating artists – Hayley Millar Baker, Maree Clarke, Dean Cross, Brad Darkson, Matthew Harris, James Howard, Jazz Money, Cassie Sullivan, this mob (Moorina Bonini, Maya Hodge, Jenna Lee, Jenna Rain Warwick and Kate ten Buuren) and Mandy Quadrio – and congratulate them for their inspiring, thought-provoking and moving work.

We are especially grateful to the Yalingwa Directions Circle who ensure that the program continues to be informed and led by First Peoples, and that their knowledge, philosophical thinking, cultural practices and protocols are embedded in this initiative. We are fortunate to be generously guided by Aunty Joy Murphy Wandin AO (Chair), Kylie Belling, Belinda Briggs, Hetti Perkins, Hannah Presley and Stacie Piper, and we thank them sincerely for their inspiring leadership, advocacy and advice.

Alongside the curatorial essay by Jessica Clark, illuminating the complex intellectual, material and cultural intersections drawn upon within and between the artists in the exhibition, we extend our appreciation to catalogue essayist Tina Baum for her important contribution to the *Between Waves* publication, foregrounding the significance of Indigenous expressions and practices of the Southeast; alongside Natalie Harkin who provides a moving poetic response to the project.

We would like to especially acknowledge the generous commitment by our Presenting Partner Creative Victoria in the establishment of the Yalingwa Initiative, and the significant contributions of Kylie Belling, Sarah Bond and Rochelle Duke from the wonderful First Peoples team. *Between Waves* has been supported by Exhibition Donor Craig Semple, as well as Exhibition Partners Fed Square, The Ian Potter Foundation, Jackson Clements Burrows Architects, NETS Victoria, Dulux; and Media Partner 3RRR; to whom we are especially grateful, along with ACCA's loyal and precious donors whose support amplifies the ambition and achievement of our programs. We equally acknowledge our valued Curatorial Symposium Partner Annamila; and Visions Australia as Touring Partner.

We extend our thanks to ACCA's team who has supported the development and presentation of this exhibition and associated programs and events with professionalism and dedication. I would like to particularly acknowledge ACCA's Exhibitions Manager Samantha Vawdrey, along with ACCA's wonderful installation team, for bringing the exhibition to life with such dedication and finesse.

We are excited to present the exhibition to our audiences at ACCA, and beyond, and are delighted that it will embark on tour across the south-eastern states of our nation. We look forward to the lively conversations and cultural insights that the exhibition will inevitably produce, and we thank and congratulate all involved for their inspiring contributions and engagement.

Max Delany
Artistic Director & CEO

Between Waves
Jessica Clark

Between Waves amplifies concepts related to light, time and vision – and the idea of shining a light on our times – expressed by the Wurundjeri Woi Wurrung word Yalingwa. The exhibition presents ten new commissions that variously explore the visible and invisible energy fields and flows set in motion by these ideas. Through a range of contemporary artforms – including video, installation, poetry, projection, photography, painting, sculpture, sound, printmaking, and a digital commission – participating artists have developed reflective and site-responsive projects that explore and experiment with the intersections of material and immaterial realms of knowledge and knowing. Collectively, works of art by Maree Clarke, Brad Darkson, Dean Cross, Matthew Harris, James Howard, Hayley Millar Baker, Jazz Money, Cassie Sullivan, this mob, and Mandy Quadrio, illuminate an interconnected web of shapeshifting ecologies within, beyond, and between what can be seen.

The exhibition has evolved alongside conversations with artists through the development of their new commissions, that centred ideas and reflections on lived experiences and materiality in relation to the exhibition's key themes of light, time, and vision. These conversations revealed the interrelationships and interactions between the articulation of these things…

> Light, a natural agent and element that stimulates sight and makes things visible/provides light or lighting to illuminate or ignite; start burning.
>
> Time, the indefinite, non-linear and multidimensional durational progress of existence and events in the past, present and future.
>
> Vision, the faculty or state of seeing, and the ability to think about or plan the future with imagination or wisdom.

While light can stimulate sight and is said to reveal truth, it can also blind, and obscure. Equally, while darkness can conceal and denote uncertainty, it can also be comforting. Between the light and the dark, in the in-between places and spaces that no one wants to venture, truth seemingly lingers; rippling inward and outward, above and below the surface. In response, the artists' featured in *Between Waves* ruminate over notions of light, time, and vision in rhythm with waves of memory and meaning that reflect, absorb and transmit in varying ways. Our yarns also centred Yorta Yorta artist Lin Onus' 'hope' that his contemporary art practice be recognised as a 'bridge between cultures, between technology, and ideas'.[1] Additionally, underpinning the exhibition is the idea of material memory; how materiality remembers place. This idea also considers the histories, stories and knowledges embedded within objects, the relationship between artists and the materials with which they choose to work, and the meaning ascribed through experience.

Beyond the scope: Maree Clarke and Brad Darkson

The site on which the Australian Centre for Contemporary Art (ACCA) now stands was once host to an expansive wetland ecosystem filled with *Phragmites australis,* more commonly known as river reeds. This environment has since been replaced by an urban landscape, though the river reeds that once stood here, are still deeply embedded within the sedimentary layers beneath the surface. In response, Maree Clarke's new commission navigates intersections and interconnections between art, culture and science. Informed by recent research in collaboration with the University of Melbourne Histology Platform, Clarke has collected thousands of microscopic images – 297 of which feature in *Between Waves* – that reveal the internal worlds and structures of river reeds, 'the extraordinary complexity of the micro realm'.[2]

Assembled as a collection of acetate prints en masse, Clarke's microscopic views of river reeds generate a multi-coloured pattern across the gallery wall in a grided formation that shifts and changes depending on viewpoint.[3] This pattern expands as the intricate and translucent imagery interacts with the light; reflecting the microscopic realm and highlighting their collective presentation within a multi-linear and interconnected network and/or ecology. now you see me: seeing the invisible #1 has also been transformed into an animated projection now you see me: seeing the invisible #2 2023. Featured at Federation Square, the pavement of which rests on a significant sacred ceremonial site for the five clans of the Kulin Nation, now you see me: seeing the invisible #2 expands the exhibition beyond ACCA's walls.[4] The work overlooks the ancient rock remnants of the once free-flowing Yarra Falls that were blown-up in 1883 by colonists to create a turning circle for ships.[5]

> 'How did we get here? Rewind to the beginning'.[6]

Brad Darkson's waiting for *kakirra* 2023 is a motion-activated two-channel work that unfolds across two large screens. Projected on the wall is a geographically mapped and 3D animated render of Kangkarratinga (also Congeratinga),[7] a site on Kaurna Country that is host to evidence of an ancient fish trap, now in pieces scattered along the shoreline. This site has recently transformed because of the recent development of a marina, and the fish trap has been destroyed. The physical presence of the audience triggers the work into action; the floor projection gradually re-builds this trap, animating and retrieving one rock at a time and bringing them together again in their intended formation. *waiting for kakirra* begins and/or continues to build only when people are present because 'you need bodies, you need many hands to build a fish trap'.[8]

Through consultation, listening and yarning with Elders on Country Darkson uncovered a Kaurna word Kurlannanaintyerlo (pronounced gerlan-anch-elo), translated by Kaurna Elder Aunty Lynnette Crocker to mean, 'curl up that sea, on the crest of a wave; Creation is in the now'.[9] The resonance between Kurlannanaintyerlo and the exhibition title, as seemingly interlinked and interchangeable terms is serendipitous and emphasises human and non-human ecologies as interconnected and working together. *waiting for kakirra* foregrounds the community work that continues to rehabilitate important cultural sites like Kangkarratinga. Central to this work is the intention to highlight the significance, complexity and legacy of First Nations aquaculture infrastructure.[10] Alongside this is a critique on ideas of progress, ignorance around ecological catastrophe and humanity's search for 'technological collaborations' to 'extend our survival'.[11] As Darkson notes, 'ignore the present. Forget the past. The rocks remain unmoved. Waiting, as kakirra passes overhead'.[12]

Beneath the surface: Matthew Harris and Mandy Quadrio

For *Between Waves* Matthew Harris has created a suite of seven large white ochre and charcoal paintings, the size and scale of which are reflective of a standard museum storage shelf. *Consigned to oblivion* 2023 depicts a series of shelves filled with rows of white archival boxes, their contents unclear. Harris' paintings formally reference notions of minimalism and seriality to draw attention to the relentless and repetitive efforts of museums and collecting institutions, and their history of gate-keeping that has denied Aboriginal ancestral remains and cultural obejcts the right to return to home. This new body of work emphasises the role of contemporary art practice in shedding light on this dark and macabre history that has been shrouded in secrecy. It is also important to note that this new work by Harris is a deeply considered and culturally sensitive response to personal experience.

Consigned to oblivion interrogates western institutions and systems that enable the fetishisation, accumulation, control and display of Indigenous sacred art and cultural objects, and ancestors who have historically been (and often seemingly still are) treated as objects; framed as a relic, 'a pitstop on the road to modern human... a missing link'.[13] Even though there has been an ongoing inquiry into the repatriation of Aboriginal ancestral remains and cultural objects and materials, still there are tens of thousands of Aboriginal ancestral remains in museums and collections, public and private, around the world.[14] They sit and wait in what Harris describes as 'institutional limbo [...] behind layers of impenetrable bureaucratic control'.[15] As an act of reclamation, reflection and care, Harris has gently layered each archival box individually in white ochre – often reserved for sorry business – framing them with a charcoal void; the remnants of a fire that ignite hope for transformation.

> 'The ongoing mistelling of Australian history manifests as a cultural amnesia'[16]

Not Gone! 2023 by Mandy Quadrio is a kinetic installation that features three suspended amorphous sculptural forms that billow outward and upward. Quadrio has stretched, wound and layered lengths of steel wire-mesh with varying levels of intervention and material manipulation. The steel wire-mesh forms are each attached to a rotating mechanism that is set in a subtle and slow-moving circular motion. As both light and movement interact and activate the work, the slow and measured rotation generates an intermittent and ever-evolving shadow-world for the viewer to navigate. As the light waves meet the work's steely fibres, the materiality reflects the full colour spectrum. Presented as a collective, each sculptural form appears to levitate in the in-between spaces – between the gallery walls, floor and ceiling. Having been set in a subtle motion *Not Gone!* gives rise to a meditative space that moves in and out of focus.

Quadrio weaves experiences, memories and stories that move and change over time. Despite the lightness of being that is inherent to the materiality *Not Gone!* conveys the illusion of density and draws focus to the spaces between; weight and weightlessness, shadow and light. These material dualities are also innate within the steel wire mesh; although the steel-wire fibres might first appear smooth and sleek, on physical interaction/connection, they are rough and can pierce the skin. For Qaudrio, 'the harsh and abrasive nature of the steel-wire mesh', references the violence inflicted by acts of erasure and unhealed wounds stemming from, 'mistold and obscured histories'[17] related to her community in lutruwita/trouwerner (Tasmania) and across the country. *Not Gone!* amplifies notions of adaptability and strength, and affirms Quadrio's ancestral connections beyond time, place and space.

More than words allow: Dean Cross and Hayley Millar Baker

On who goes to The Gallows 1997-2023 is a sculptural self-portrait that draws on Dean Cross's personal and family archive of objects and materials collected since birth. Through a process guided by contemplation, Cross has brought together a collection of objects and materials that hold deep personal significance. The artists childhood yidaki rests atop two ceramic bricks that derive from a now demolished hospital building; Cross's birthplace on Ngunnawal and Ngambri Country.[18] These objects have been arranged on a recently acquired three metre long, three-tier aluminium bleacher; the heart of the work.[19] *On who goes to The Gallows* reflects on the conflicting waves of memory and meaning ascribed to objects, which are encoded and evolved over time. While the bleacher conveys dual notions of community and competition, reflection and observation, of hiding-out and meeting-up, Cross's black hoodie ascends as a symbol of resistance.

On who goes to The Gallows centres contemplation, triggered by cycles of memory and grief – the past, present and future colliding in the now. Cross prompts reflection on life, loss and learning. The term 'gallows' refers to a medieval apparatus used for execution by hanging. For me, this conjures colloquial sayings and symbols such as 'hanging by a thread', 'meeting your maker', and the 'hanged man'. In this work, Cross reflects on life stages, shifts, and changes; we are all experiencing the same time, we all go to the gallows eventually. In doing so, the work navigates ideas of presence and absence, the said and unsaid, the known and unknown, truth and assumption, life and death.

> 'Are we the sum of all our experiences? Or are we somehow something more?'[20]

Entr'acte 2023 is a new single-channel video work by Hayley Millar Baker, the title of which refers to an interlude or performance occurring between two acts of a play: in French *entre* meaning between and *acte* meaning act. The work centres a female protagonist, presented in portrait view and tightly cropped from the shoulders-up and with the frame encroaching at the edges of her face. This figure has been cast as a 'vessel' representative of 'woman' and that channels the physical and mental weight of forced emotional containment, and the subsequent build-up of energy suppressed in the body, over time. By harnessing and embodying the in-between internal moments of 'restrained rage turned to grief',[21] *Entr'acte* provides a powerful and empowering means through which to respond to and release these tensions.

Millar Baker's new commission is at once autobiographical and a social commentary. Presented in silence and at a scale larger than life, *Entr'acte* evokes and embraces notions of intensity and intimacy to examine lived and felt experiences, navigating the self and the world; and the resulting complex anxieties and expectations that stem from this. Over 11 minutes and 20 seconds, *Entr'acte* holds the moment between an action and a reaction. As the durational performance unfolds, the initial wide-eyed brightness of the protagonist gradually fades; the physical toll begins manifest. By harnessing the strength, power and focus required to navigate these moments with restraint, Millar Baker confronts audiences with an invitation to look and think inward, beneath the surface and beyond oneself.

From one state to the next: Jazz Money and James Howard

James Howard's *Subterranean frequencies* 2023 is a generative sound sculpture that explores the intersecting realms of material and immaterial experience through a multi-layered soundscape that responds to place. Howard has gathered a series of field recordings from deep within the dark cavernous space that expands benath the gallery floor; connected to the Grant Street Ventilation Stack located at the back of ACCA's north forecourt.[22] This 'Stack' is a towering bright red structure, masquerading as public art, and is linked to the network of tunnels that funnel a continual day-to-night stream of traffic. By amplifying such spaces, Howard draws attention to the often-unnoticed sights, sounds and structures of the everyday that are hidden in plain sight.

Subterranean frequencies is composed of four multi-layered soundtracks that invariably rise and fall, all with different durations: 17, 19, 23 and 29 minutes. Each layer of audio emanates from a series of directional speakers attached to a circular structure that descends from above and casts a shadow that is reminiscent of the structure of the 'Stack'. While each track begins in alignment, by design, over time they become asynchronous. Howard has calculated that it would take four months and twenty-five days for the work to complete a single loop and become realigned. By interweaving a mixture of high-pitched noises and subtle sonic resonances that are site-responsive, with breaks or 'breaths' of silence layered between, *Subterranean frequencies* highlights the way that sound can elicit emotion, despite not having a physical form itself. In doing so, Howard emphasises how time is malleable, and ever evolving as part of a continuum.

> 'Stories and histories still waiting to be heard. Is anyone receiving them?'[23]

infinite iterative piece 2023 brings together the three strands of Jazz Money's practice: poetry, installation and film. Presented across three adjoining screens, the work features an evolving poem with infinite possibilities; what Money describes as a 'digital exquisite corpse'.[24] The three visual portals that Money opens work together to connect a range of land, city, and sea scapes that collectively form an ever-evolving horizon line that is multifaceted and multidimensional. Incorporating still and moving images collected and shared throughout *infinite iterative piece,* Money reflects on lived and felt experiences travelling across the country at home, and throughout the world.[25] While the screens have been positioned alongside one another, *infinite iterative piece* generates a series of juxtaposing compositions that are ever-changing and interlinked.

Money's imagery and footage is interwoven with a series of black voids, each screen overlaid with a line of text, sometimes two, resurfaced from her personal archive of 'lost lines' from previous creative writing projects that hadn't yet found a 'home'. The layers of still and moving imagery with transitioning text appear randomly, 'neither creator nor audience know what will be revealed in any single moment'.[26] Paired with an ambient and ethereal soundscape, *infinite iterative piece* creates new experiences, that will grow and expand as more lines are added over time, repeated and replayed in an infinite loop. This approach reflects on the immense output and overload of information in the everyday, and the human desire to attempt to make sense and meaning out of it all. Within *Between Waves,* Money's new commission provides a moment of respite amidst the chaos, to slow and stop.

Beyond time and space: Cassie Sullivan and this mob

Cassie Sullivan's new commission *wayi (to hear)* 2023 includes a series of large-scale monotypes presented as a collective; a family. Each imprint is soft and subtle having been overlaid on clouded acrylic, the translucency of which conjures the mist that gathers and disperses across Country in lutruwita/trouwerner.[27] The muslin fabric that features, known as tarlatan, is an everyday malleable material of care typically used as a gauze, or to swaddle babies. Prior to printing, Sullivan has pushed and pulled large swathes of this fabric across melukerdee and nuenonne Country, across grasslands and shorelines, sandy beaches and deep within the bay where the salt and fresh water meet. Along the journey, the tarlatan has collected and embedded 'knowledge of place' within its delicate fibres, 'the language of salt and blood-stained water.'[28]

Through process and outcome, the weight of Sullivan's body, and the traces and gestures of her movements now held within the materiality, meld place-based memory, blood memory and corpereal remembering.[29] In doing so, *wayi (to hear)* conveys a deeply personal somatic language that explores the ways in which transgenerational communication and trauma moves through and is held in the body and mind, and is brought into physicality. Installed in a panoramic formation, suspended from the ceiling, *wayi (to hear)* invites moments of pause, and slow movement through; to be able to see each impression clearly the viewer must move around the edges of the installation. This visual and material ambiguity creates a network of ancestral imprinting for the viewer to navigate.

> 'Positive, negative
> present, missing
> floating, bound'[30]

For *Between Waves* this mob members Moorina Bonini, Maya Hodge, Jenna Lee, Jenna Rain Warwick and Kate ten Buuren highlight the breadth of their individual and collaborative practices through a new digital commission. Taking form as an interactive digital zine that centres notions of interactivity and connection, *Black Wattle Volume II* 2023 gathers a collection of thoughts and reflections on what it means to be connected with a blak collective and community. *this mob* weave conversations, experiences and memories that unfold through a considered process of deep listening and collective making, to map connections and disconnections with one another and the self, across time, place and space.

Black Wattle Volume II establishes a dynamic platform for connection between members, community and the world beyond the borders of the studio, state and country. Creative contributions include a new photographic series by Bonini and Lee, a short horror film by Rain Warwick, collected and collaged photographs, a new series of cyanotypes by ten Buuren, shared recipes and cook-ups by Hodge, and an interactive crossword puzzle by invited collaborator Alice Skye.[31] Bonini explains, 'the digital space becomes the interface between ourselves; a space where we can speak from'.[32] Like this mob's shared studio, *Black Wattle Volume II* carves-out time and space for listening and yarning, and for rest – to be together, to connect and make without the external pressure to produce or present.

Between Waves navigates ideas of presence and absence, the known and unknown, and transgenerational and collective consciousness. The ten ambitious new commissions traverse internal and external worlds, embracing the sensory and cyclical rhythms of light and sound, thinking and feeling, listening and seeing, alongside ideas of material memory, and forms of meaning that influence encounters with self, each other and the world. The participating artists employ a range of technologies to reflect on life cycles and shifts, to emphasise cultural, personal and social histories, which are invariably entwined with acts of remembering, rehabilitation, regeneration, and reclamation. Together, their new commissions resound a collective call for relational accountability and ethical responsibility that locates individual experience not at the centre of the world, but as an inherent part of its fabric. By embracing the push and pull dynamics that build beneath the surface, *Between Waves* reflects on the interrelationship between life, materiality, people and place, and resounds a need to find balance.

1 Lin Onus, 'Language and Lasers: Urban Aboriginal', *Blacklines: Contemporary Critical Writing by Indigenous Australians*, Michele Grossman (ed.), Melbourne University Press, Carlton, 2003, p 92-96.
2 Maree Clarke, Artist Statement, 2023.
3 Ibid.
4 The Kulin Nation consists of five language groups who are the true custodians of Naarm, what is known as the Port Phillip Region of Victoria. Kulin Nation territories extend around Port Phillip and Western Port bays, up into the Great Dividing Range and the Loddon and Goulburn River valleys. See: 'Traditional Owners & Languages of our Campuses', *Victoria University, Melbourne Australia*, https://www.vu.edu.au/about-vu/university-profile/moondani-balluk-indigenous-academic-unit/acknowledging-country/traditional-owners-languages-of-our-campuses.
5 The Yarra Falls used to stretch across the Birrarung (Yarra River) where Queen Street is located today. It was demolished through the use of dynamite by colonists in 1883 to make way for ships to turn. See: Museum of Lost Things, The Yarra Waterfall, https://www.museumoflost.com/the-yarra-waterfall/.
6 Brad Darkson, Artist Statement, 2023.
7 Kangkarratinga or Congeratinga is a Kaurna word that means, where the river meets the ocean. Brad Darkson in conversation with author, 29 June 2023.
8 Brad Darkson in conversation with author, 29 June 2023.
9 Aunty Lynette Crocker in conversation with Brad Darkson, 5 June 2023.
10 The process of making Brad Darkson's new commission has been informed by Community consultation with Narungga and local Kaurna community members including ngangki burka senior Kaurna woman Aunty Lynette Crocker, Aunty Merle Simpson and Uncle Jeffrey Newchurch.
11 Darkson, 2023.
12 Ibid.
13 The trade of Aboriginal ancestral remains was fuelled by scientific racist theories, that appropriated Charles Darwin's theory of evolution to justify Western (white) society's hierarchical position as the most evolved. In an attempt to prove, that Aboriginal people were the least evolved, this macabre and deluded theory was used to justify the theft, abuse and sale of Aboriginal ancestral remains to museum collections and private collectors in Australia, and around the world.
14 Bob Weatherall, in conversation with Warraba Weatherall, keynote, 'Purrumpa: First Nations Arts & Culture Gathering', Adelaide, 31 October - 4 November 2022.
15 Matthew Harris, Artist Statement, 2023.
16 Mandy Quadrio, Artist Statement, 2023.
17 Quadrio, 2023.
18 Dean Cross in conversation with the author, 23 May 2023.
19 Bleachers such as this one, typically function as seating for spectatorship, often encountered in school yards, at community and/or sporting events.
20 Dean Cross in conversation with author, 23 May 2023.
21 Hayley Millar Baker, Artist Statement, 2023.
22 The Grant Street Ventilation Stack is located at ACCA's north forecourt. It is a functional tower structure that only activates when an accident occurs in the Burnley Tunney network to release smoke build-up and ensure visibility for drivers.
23 Jazz Money, Artist Statement, 2023.
24 James Howard, Artist Statement, 2023.
25 Photographic images and video footage from Jazz Money's recent travels in Australia, USA, Lebanon, Palestine, India, and Italy feature throughout *infinite iterative piece*.
26 Money, 2023.
27 Cassie Sullivan, Artist Statement, 2023.
28 Ibid.
29 Blood memory relates to intergenerational trauma stored and experienced in the body through DNA; having been passed on and transmitted across time and space. Body memory can be understood as the sum of all past bodily experiences that are stored in memory and influence behaviour. See: Antje Gentsch and Esther Kuehn, 'Clinical Manifestations of Body Memories: The Impact of Past Bodily Experiences on Mental Health', *Brain Sciences Journal*, Michael Schaefer (ed), Multidisciplinary Digital Publishing Institute, issue 12.5, 2002, accessed 28 June 2023, https://www.ncbi.nlm.nih.gov/pmc/articles/PMC9138975/#:~:text=Conceptually%2C%20body%20memory%20is%20defined,as%20well%20as%20accompanying%20emotions.
30 Sullivan, 2023.
31 Moorina Bonini, Jenna Rain Warwick and Maya Hodge's creative contributions were developed during this mob's recent residency facilitated by Agency AiR in collaboration with InPace, the Garambi Baan/Laughing Waters Residency Centre that operates in partnership with the Wurundjeri Woi-Wurrung Cultural Heritage Aboriginal Corporation and Parks Victoria to support culture, arts, research and science.
32 Moorina Bonini (this mob), Artist Statement, 2023.

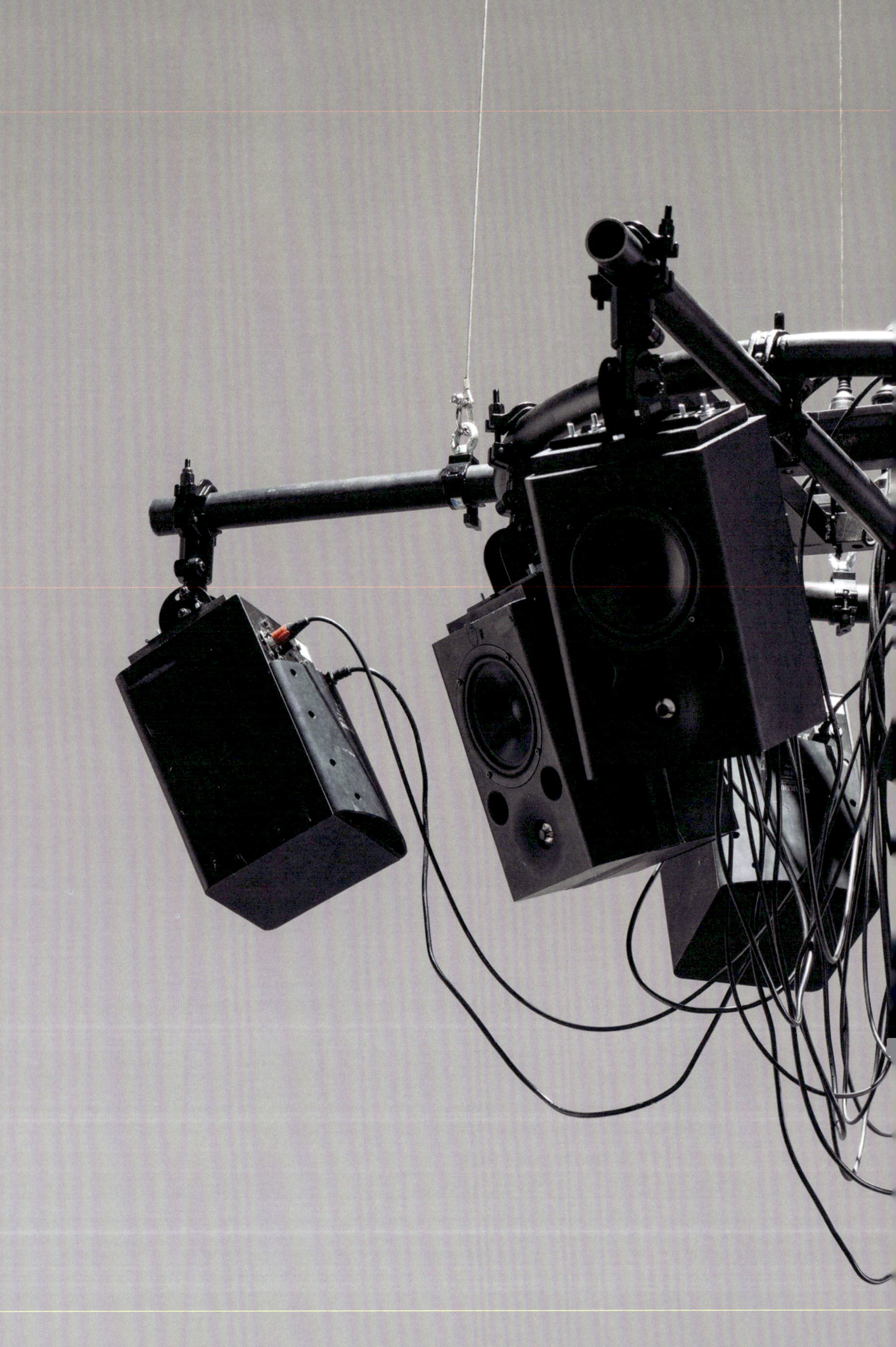

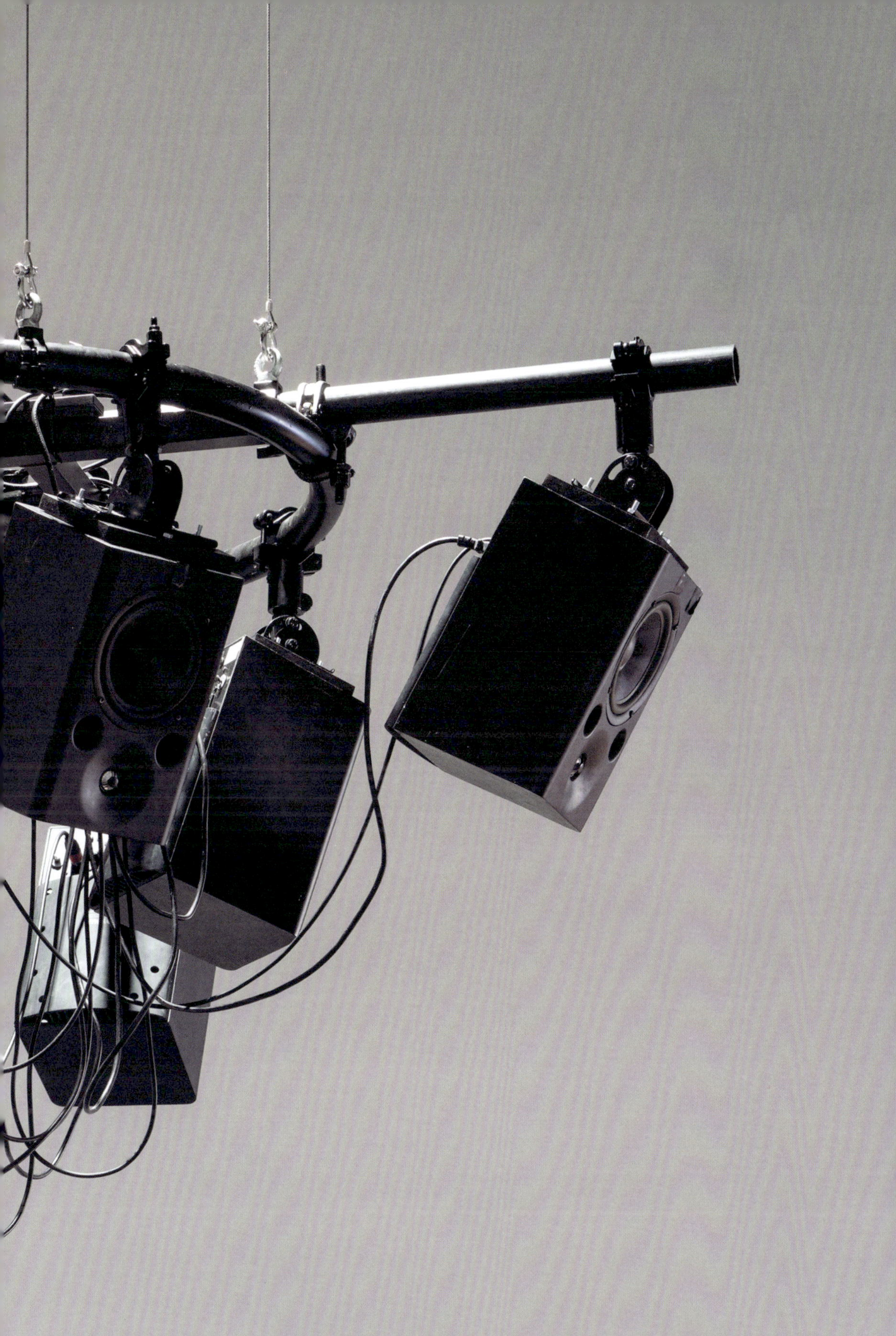

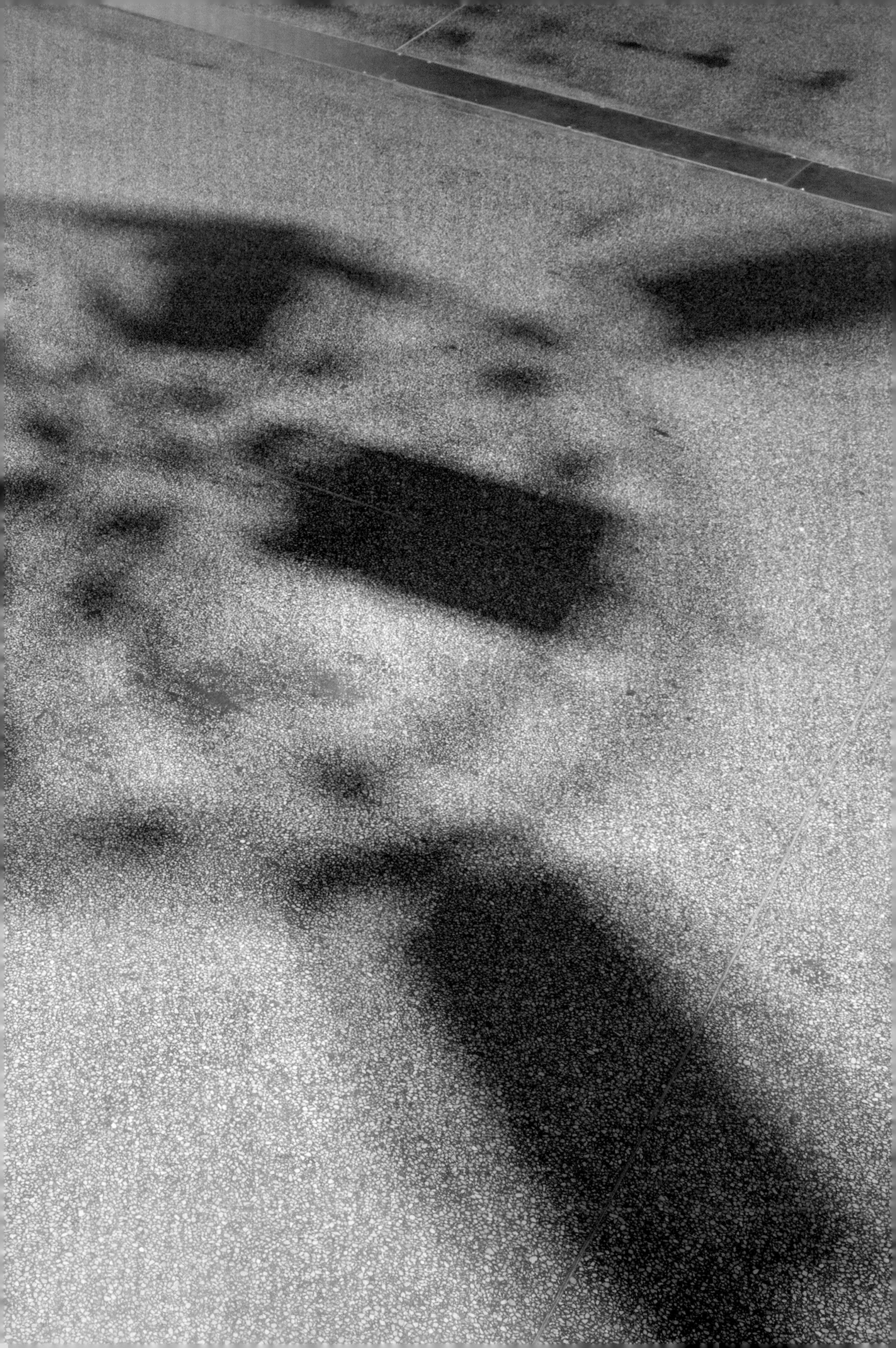

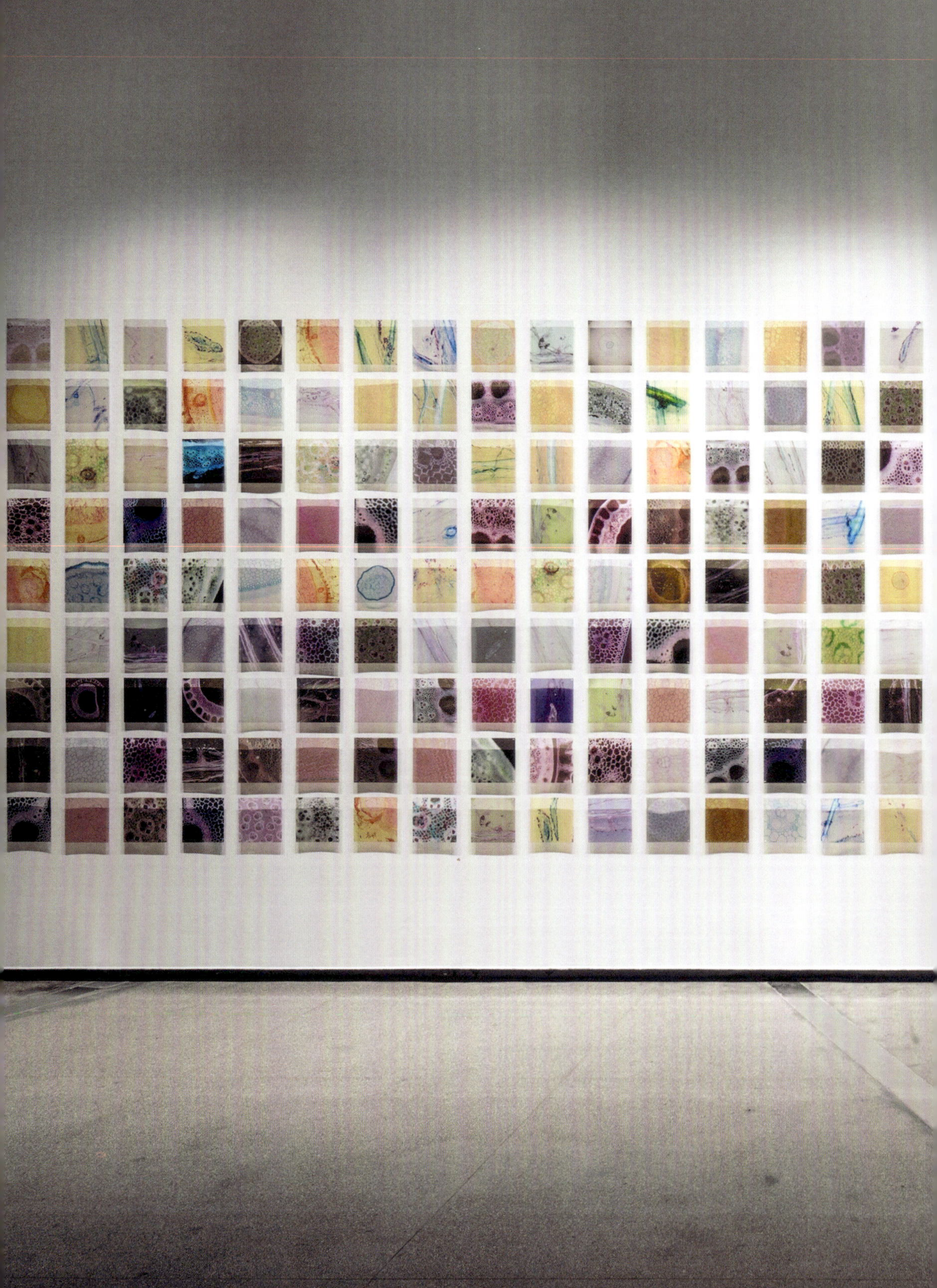

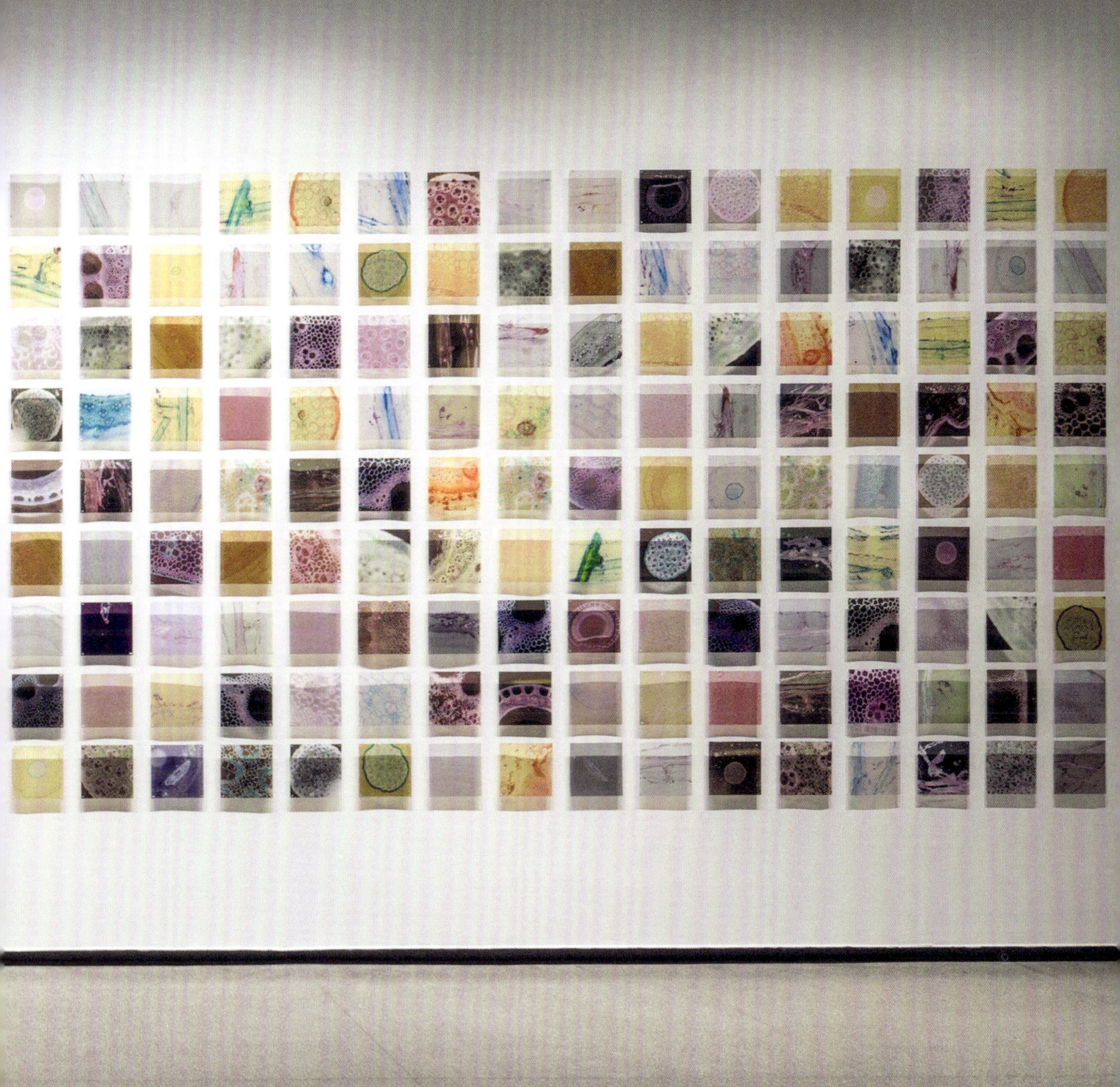

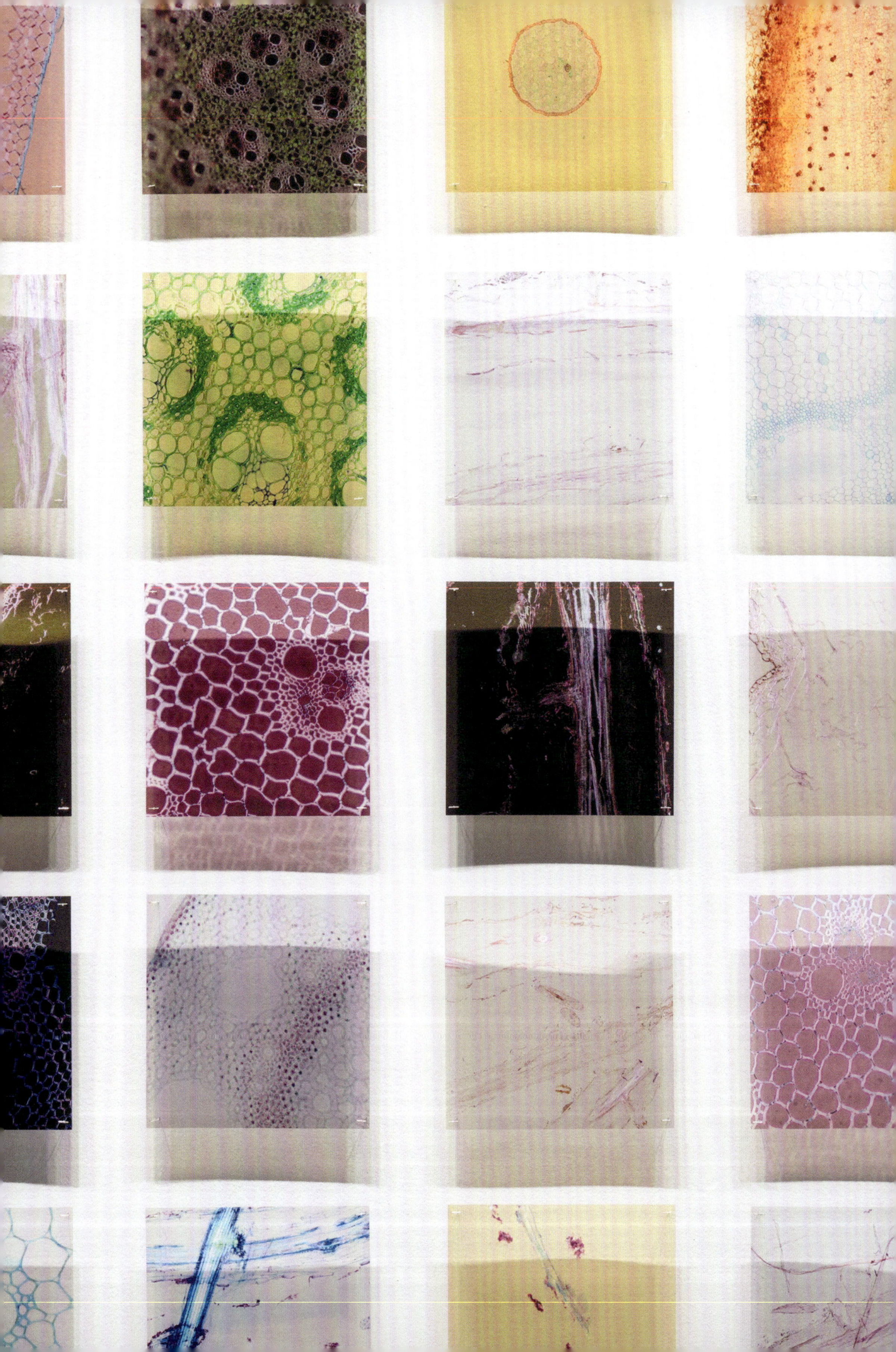

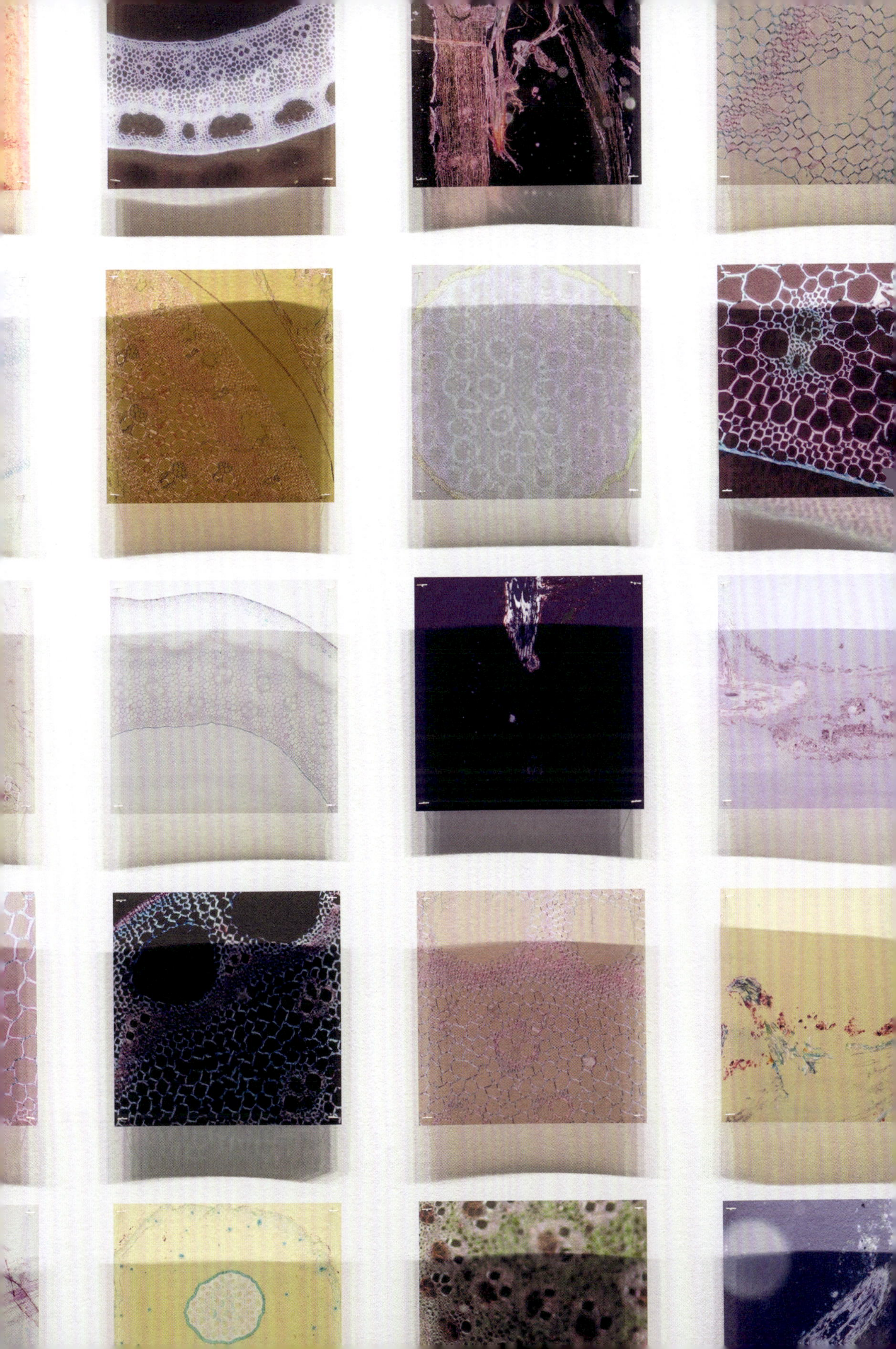

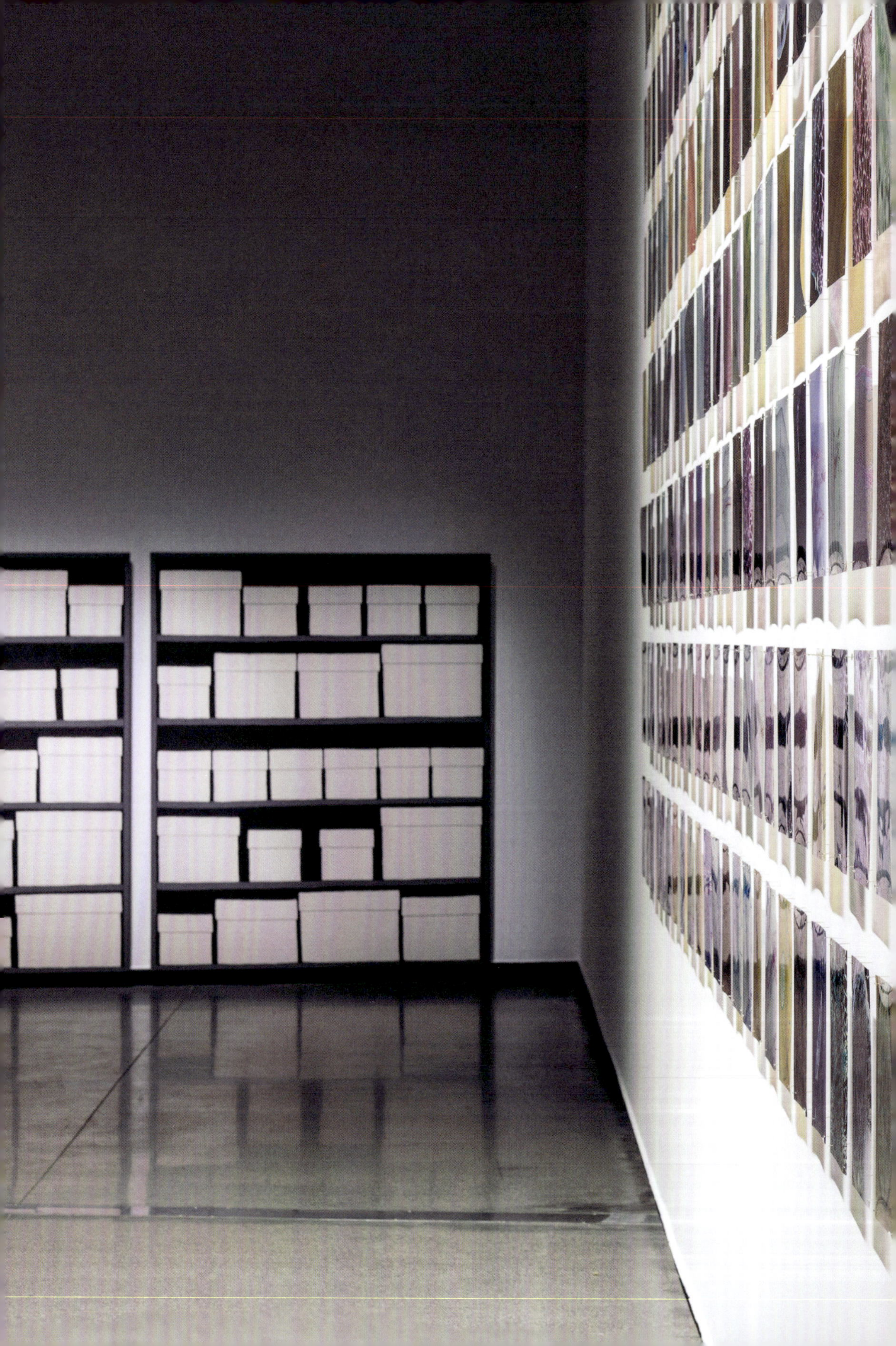

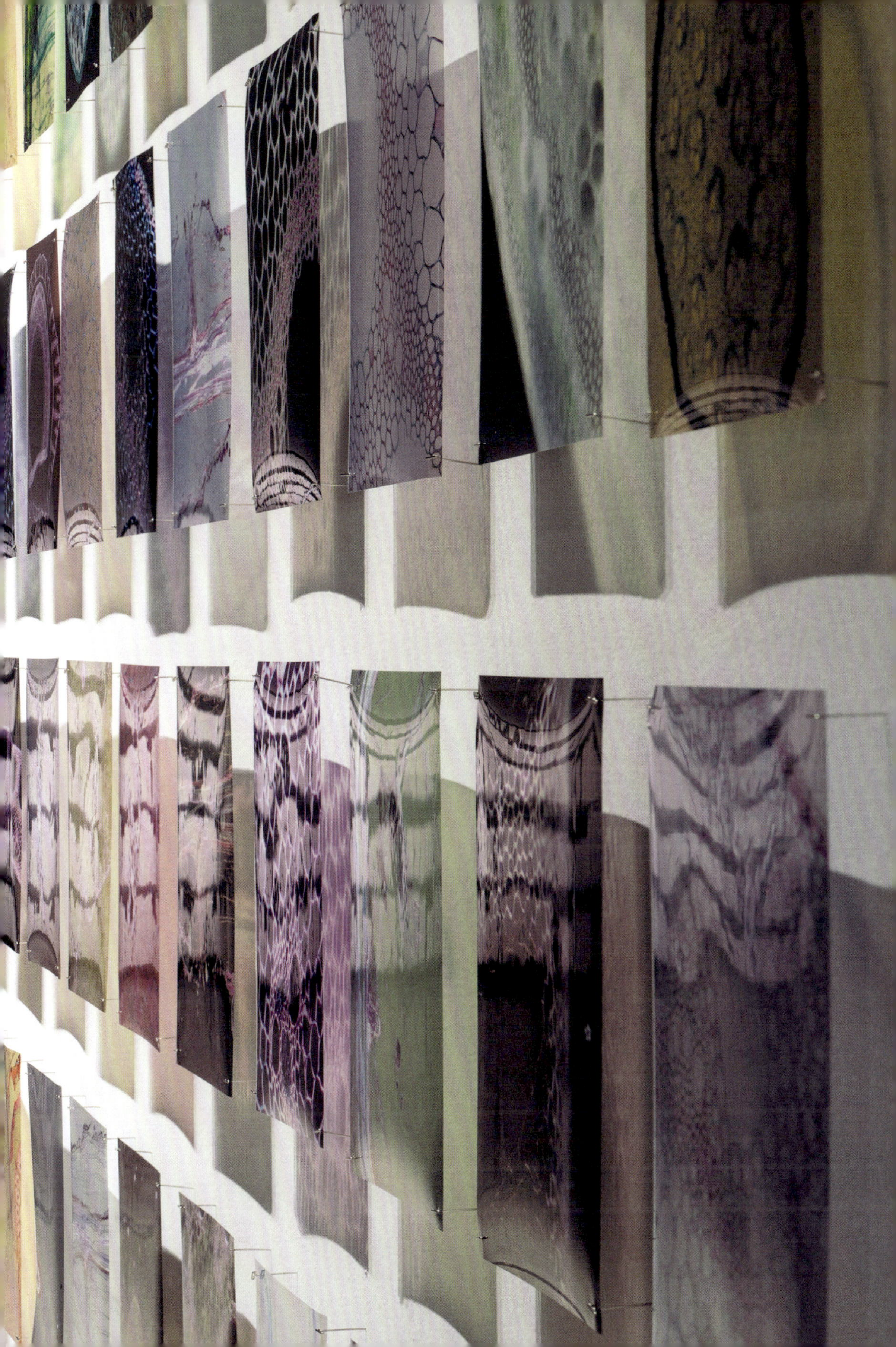

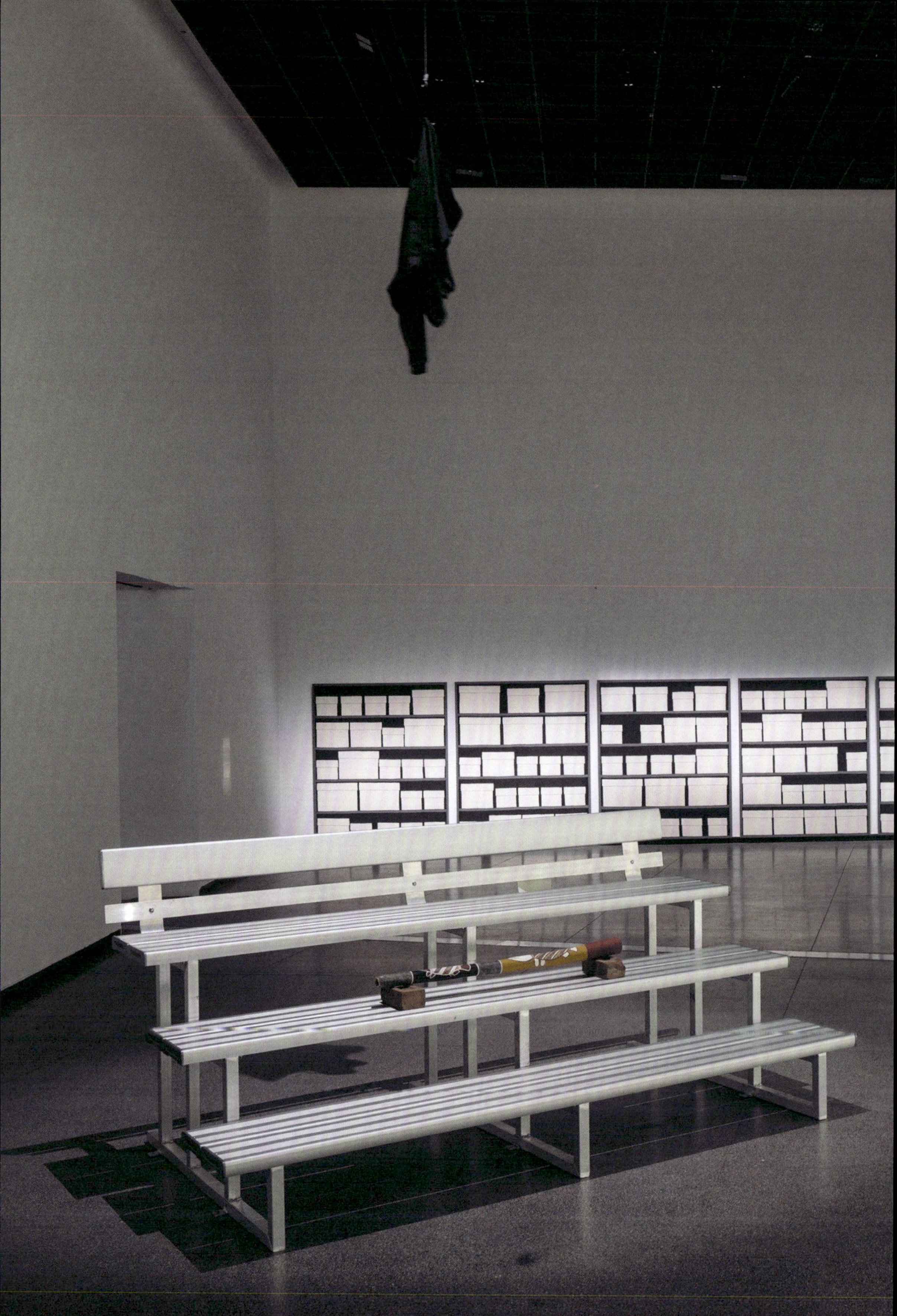

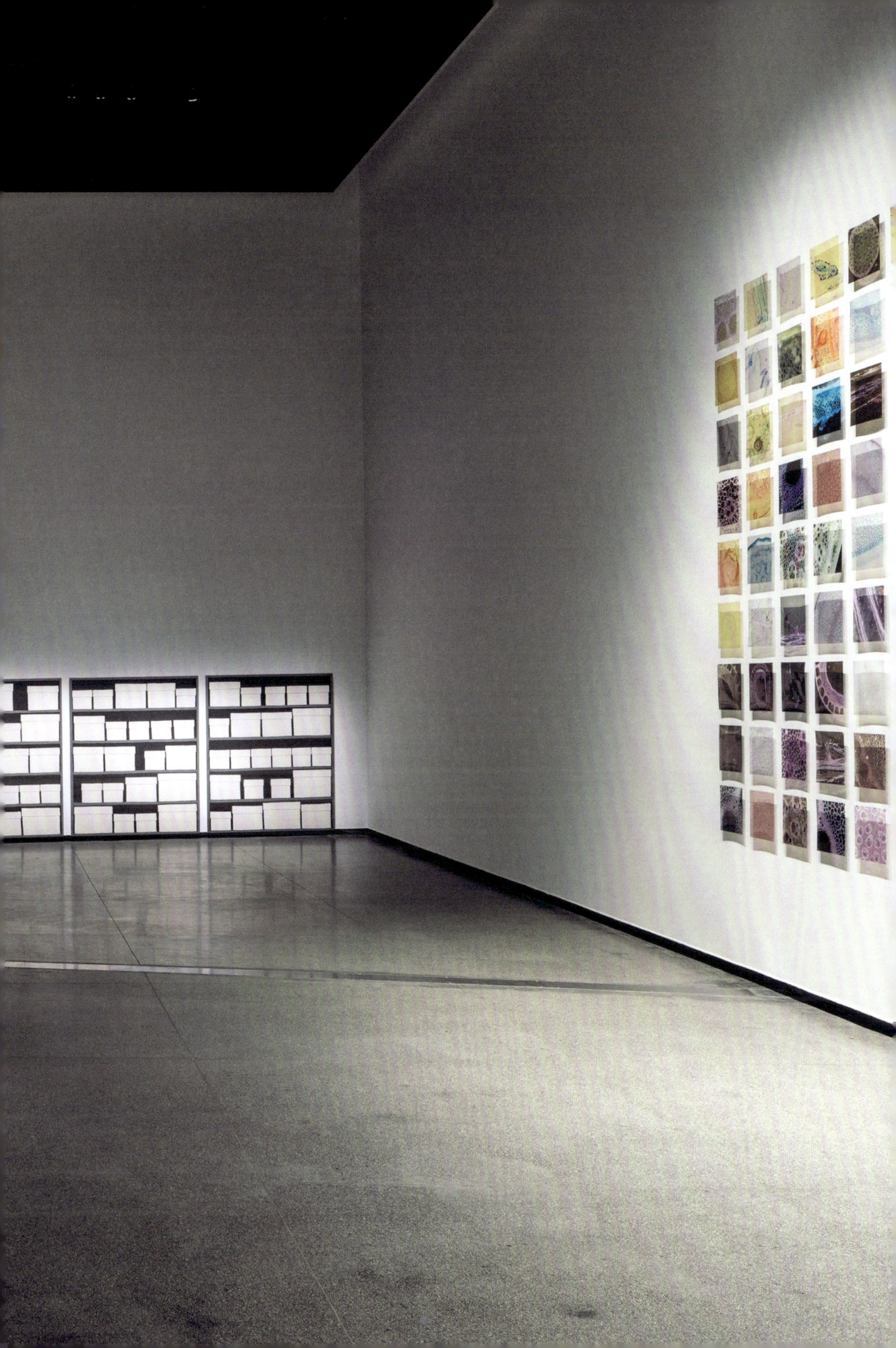

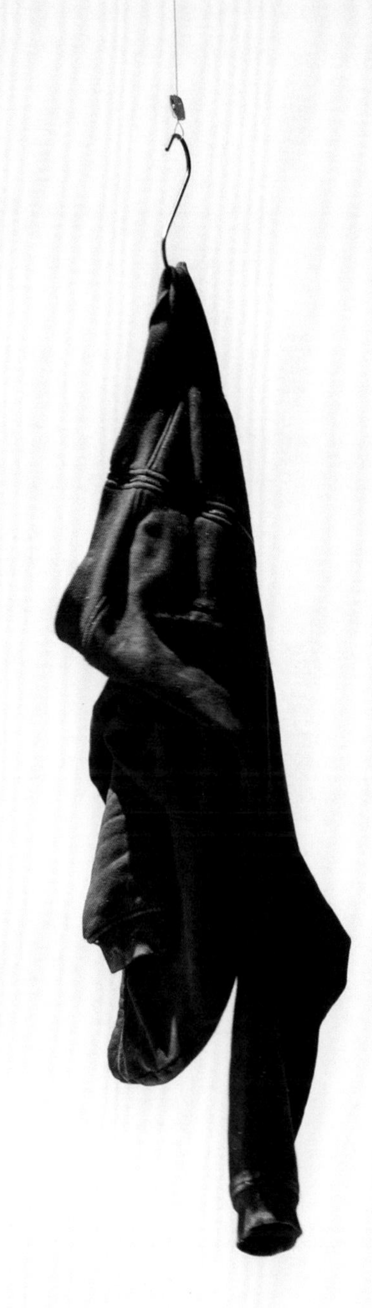

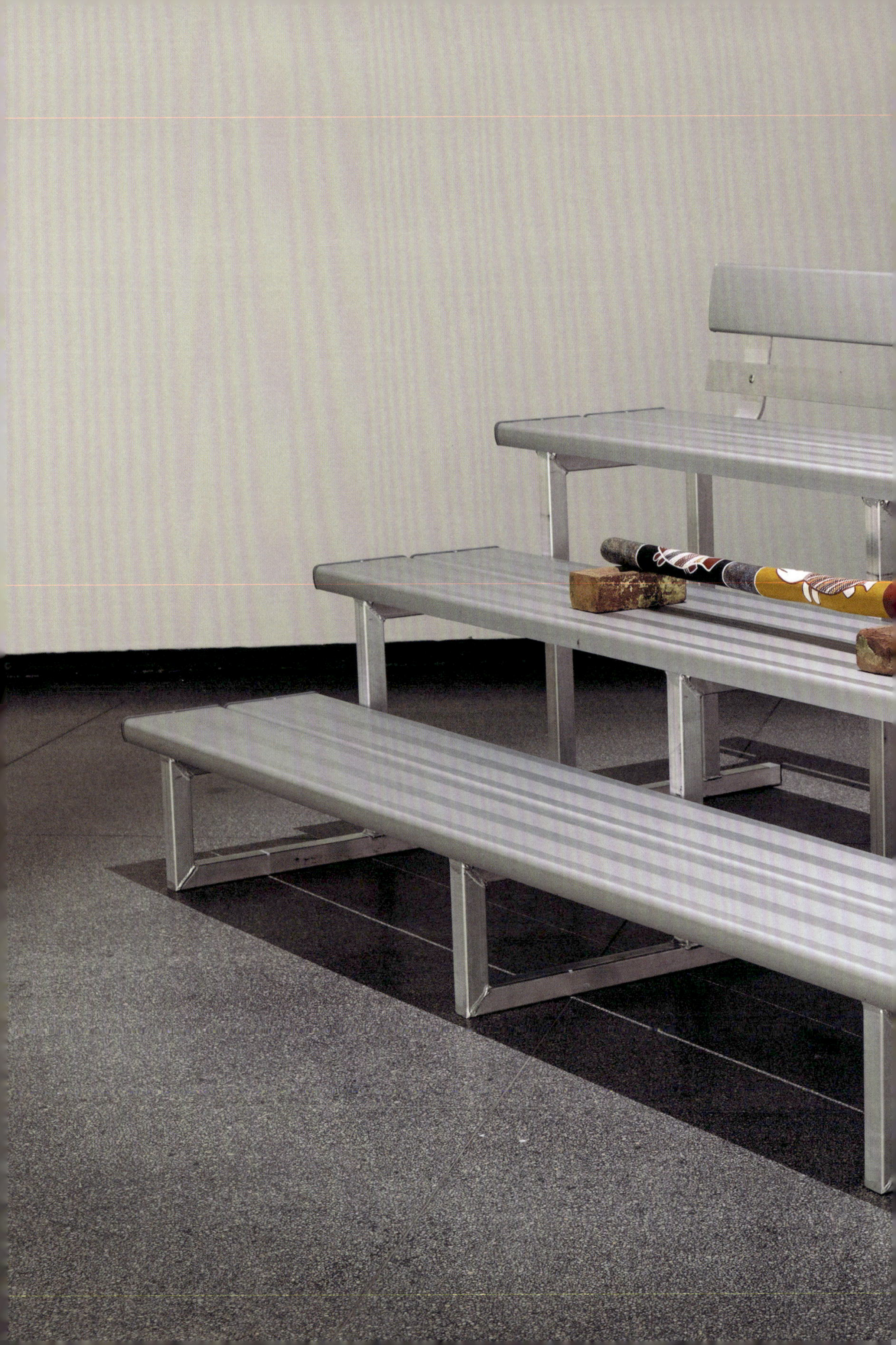

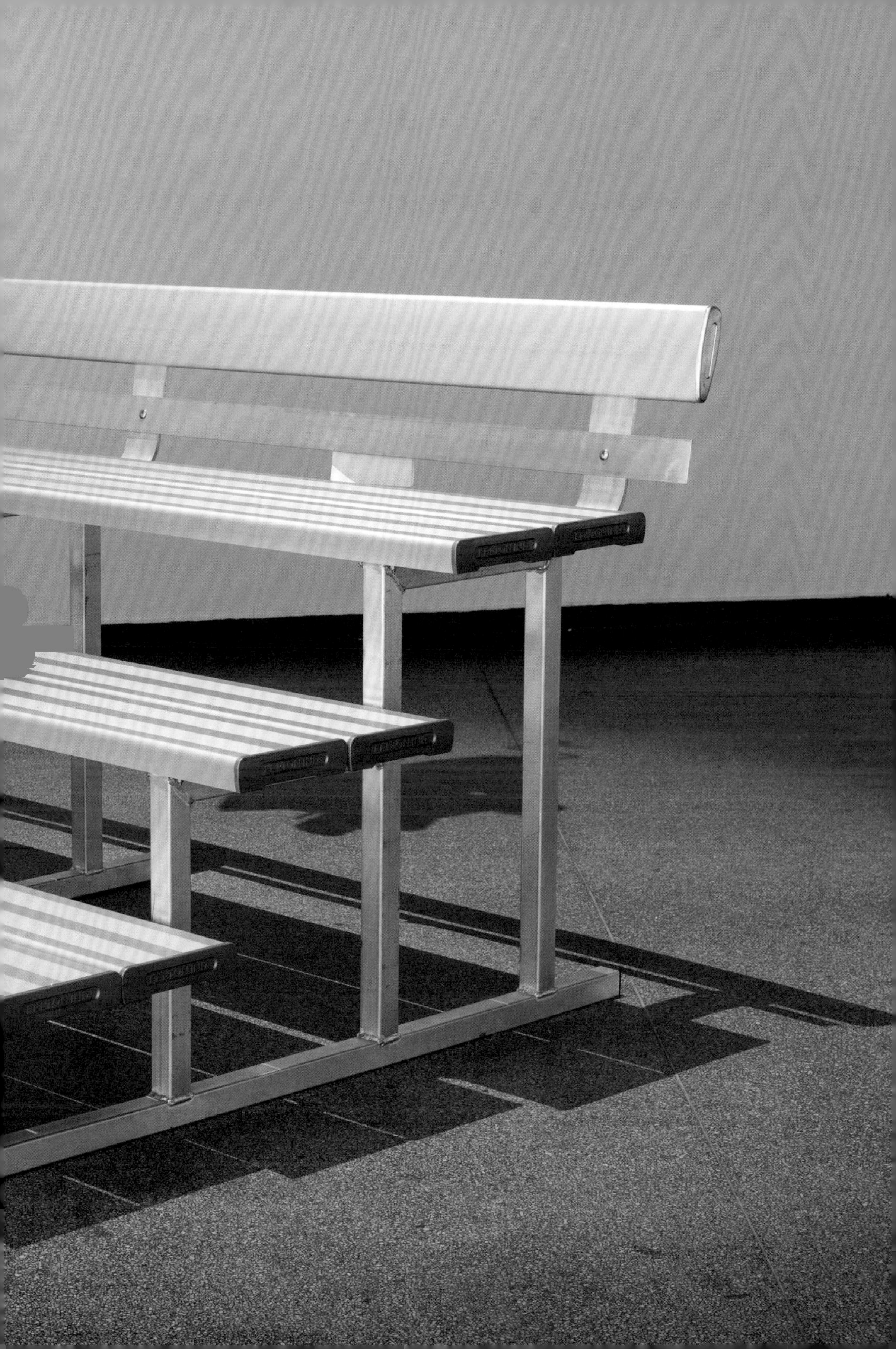

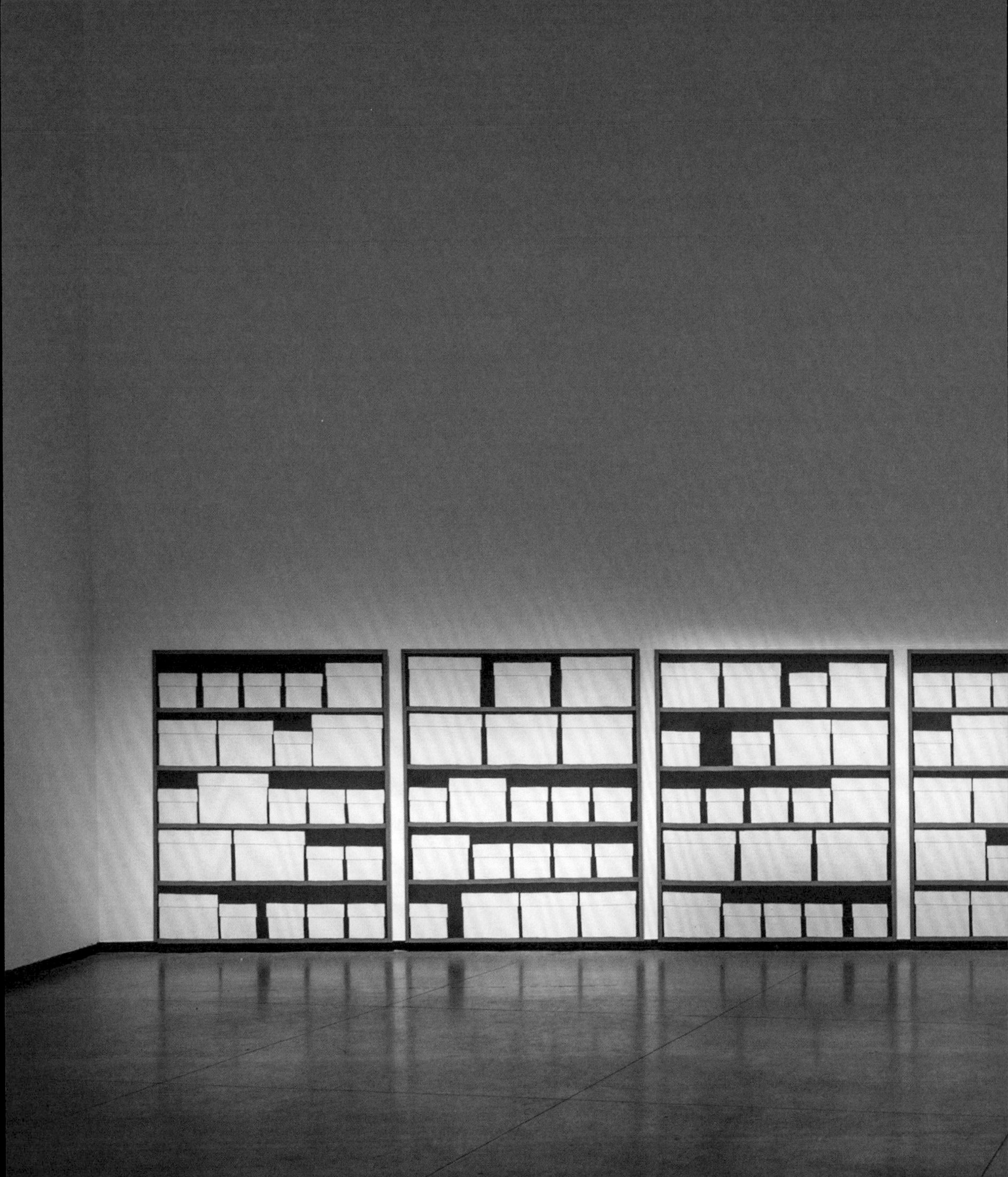

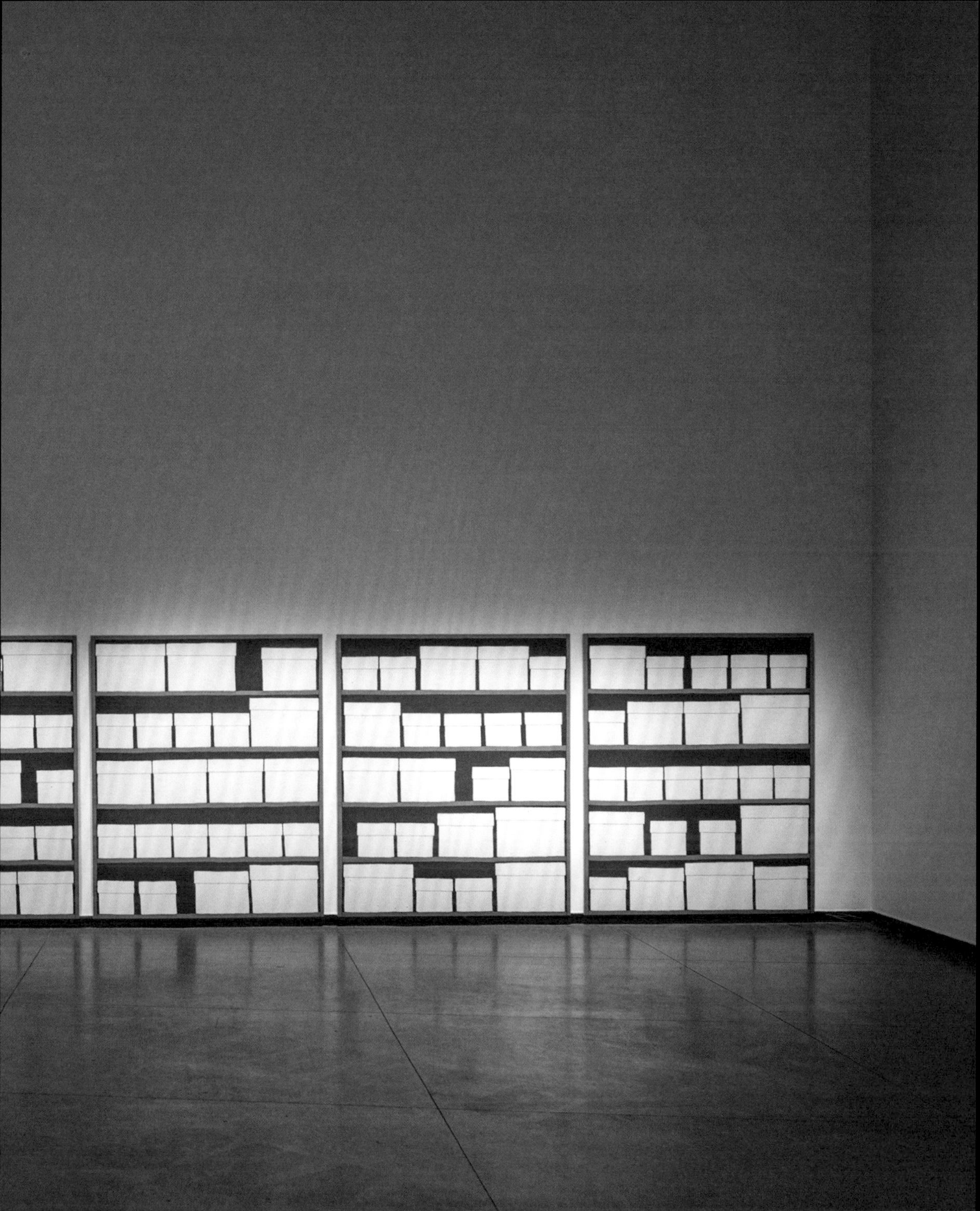

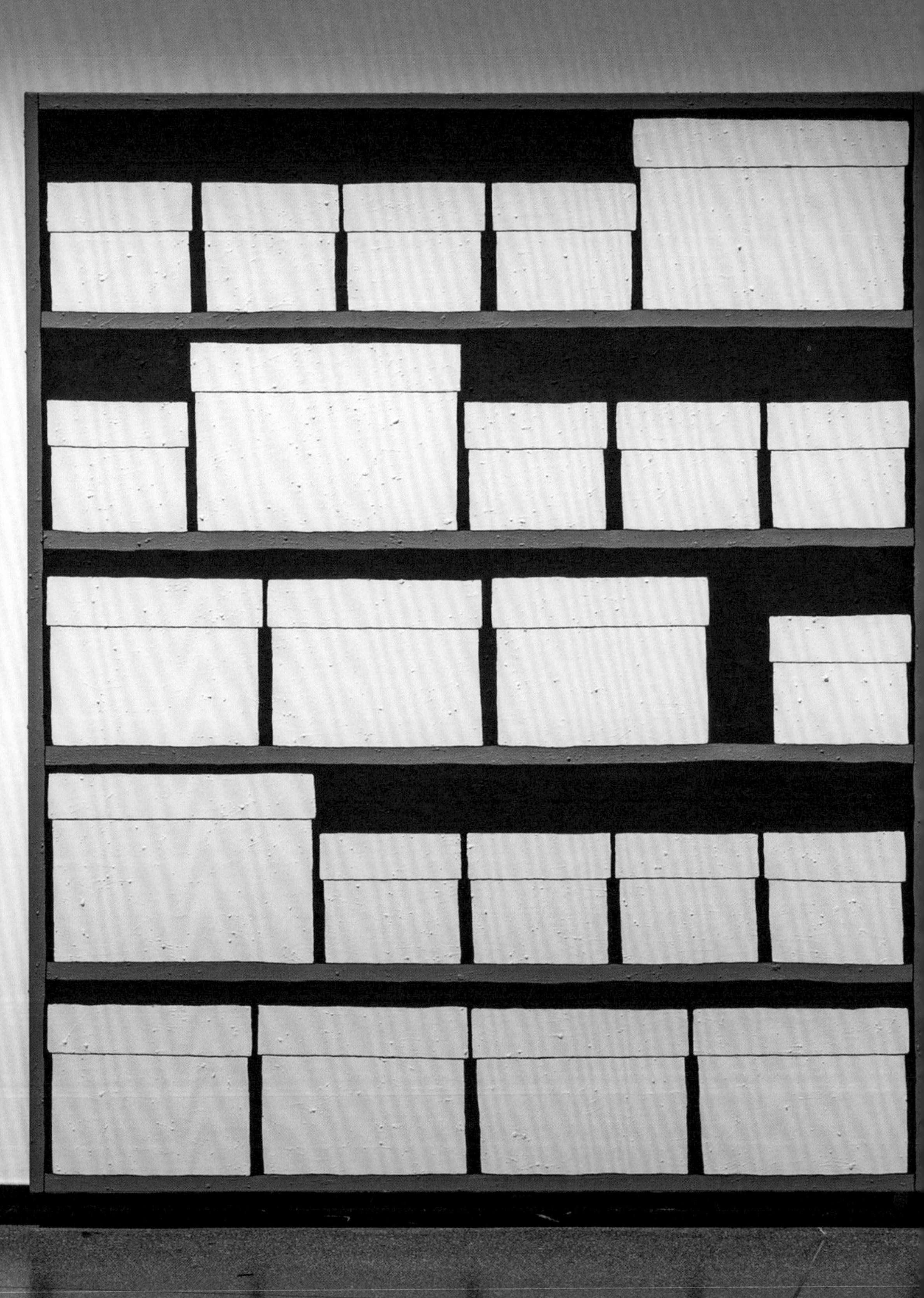

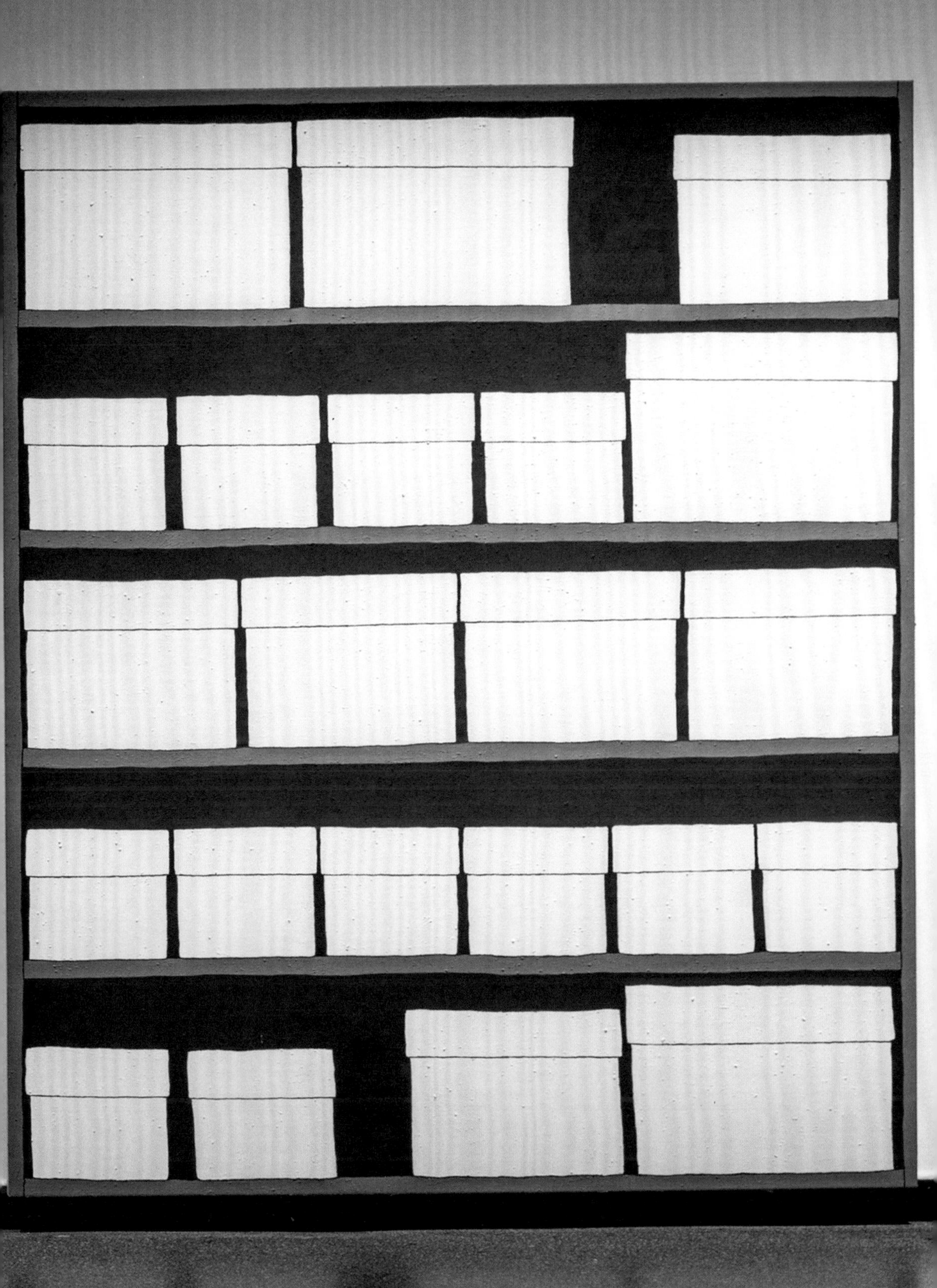

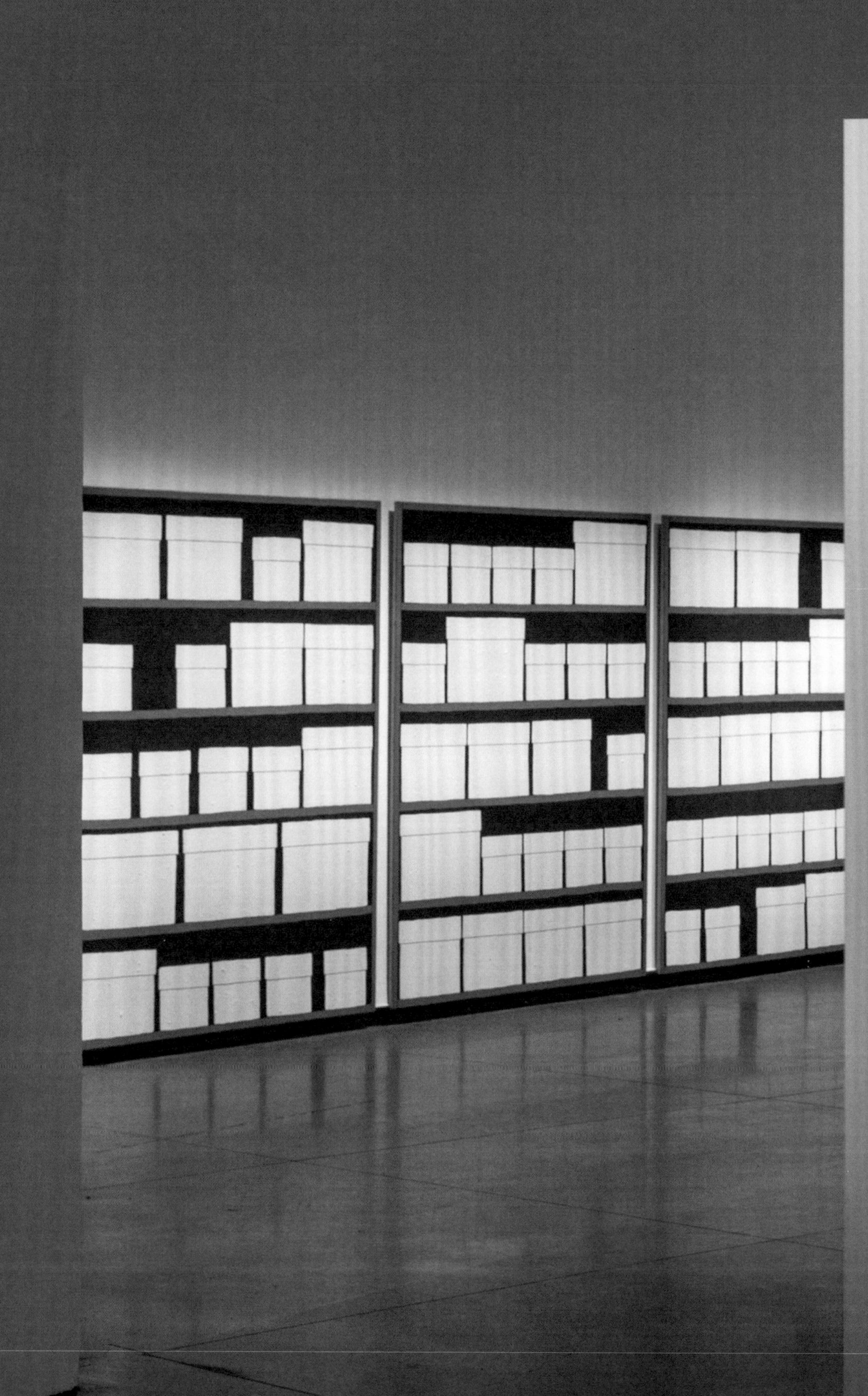

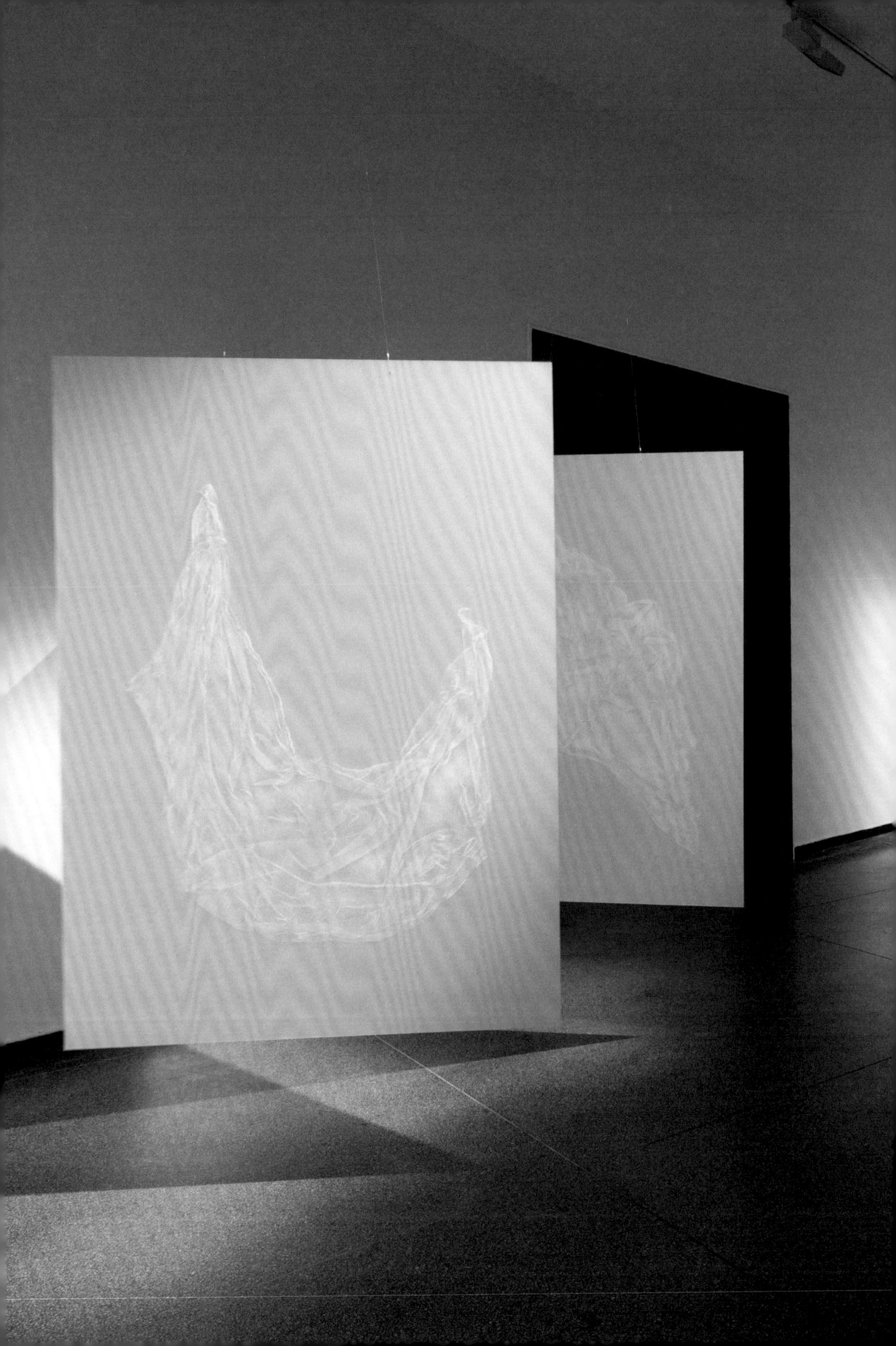

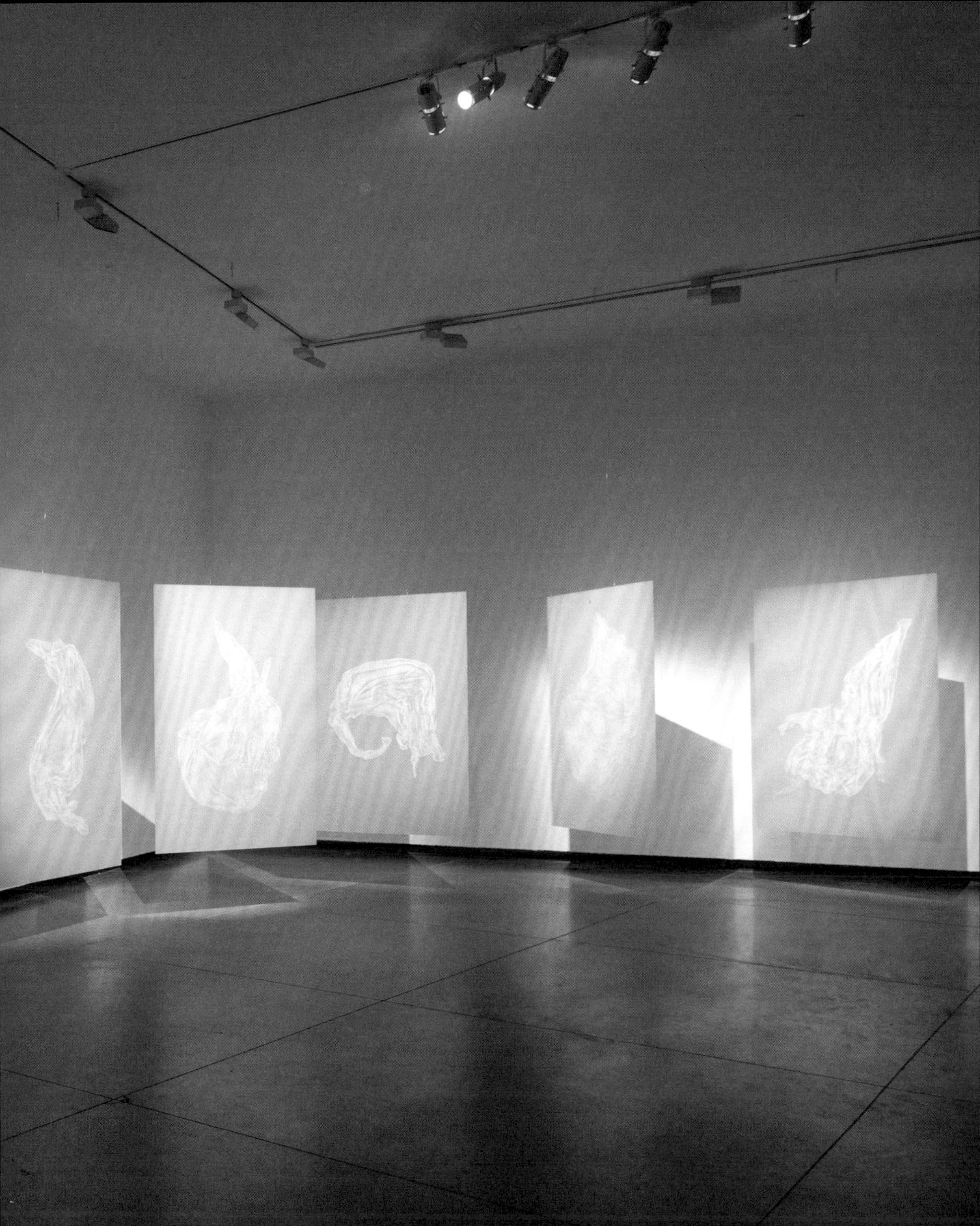

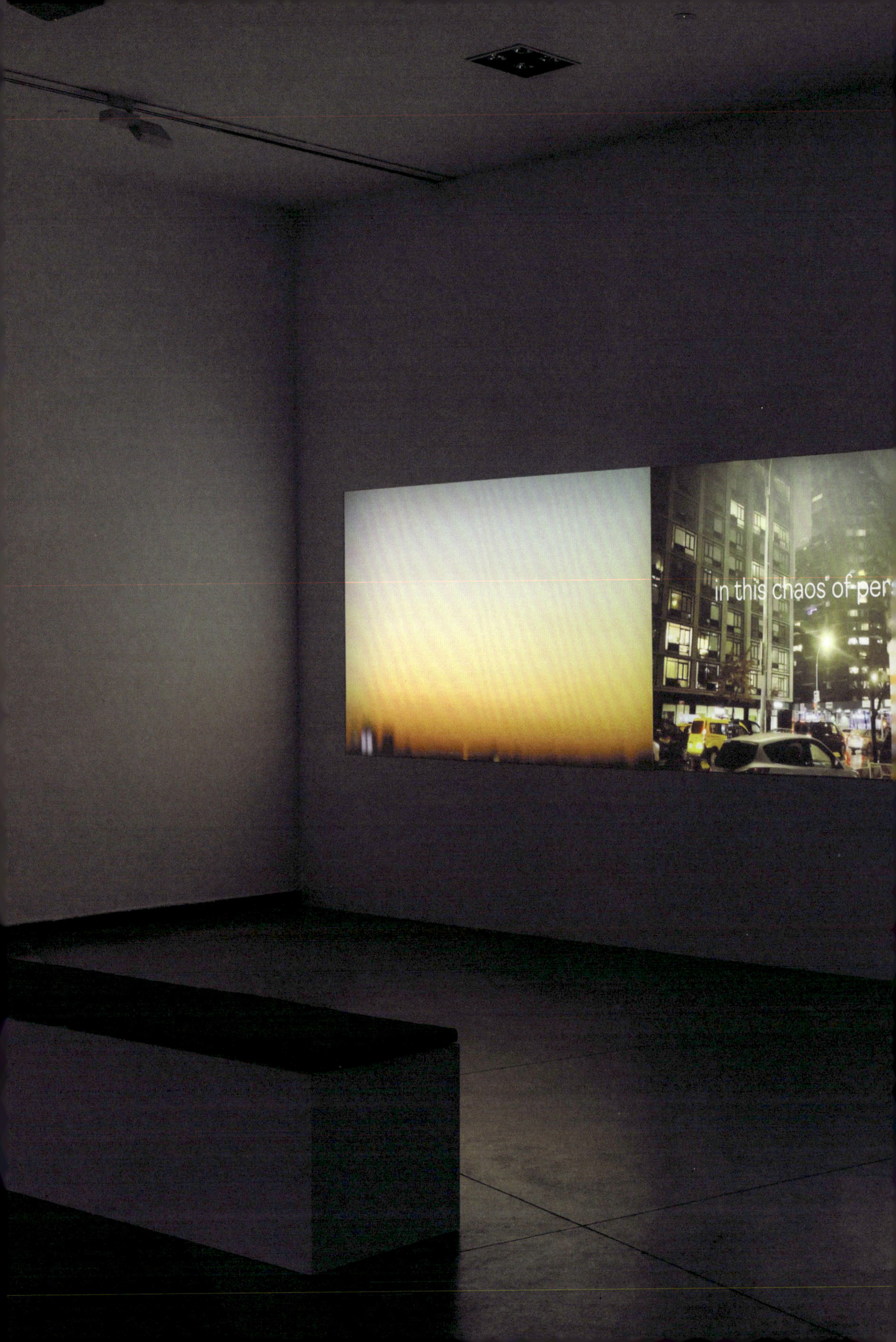
in this chaos of per

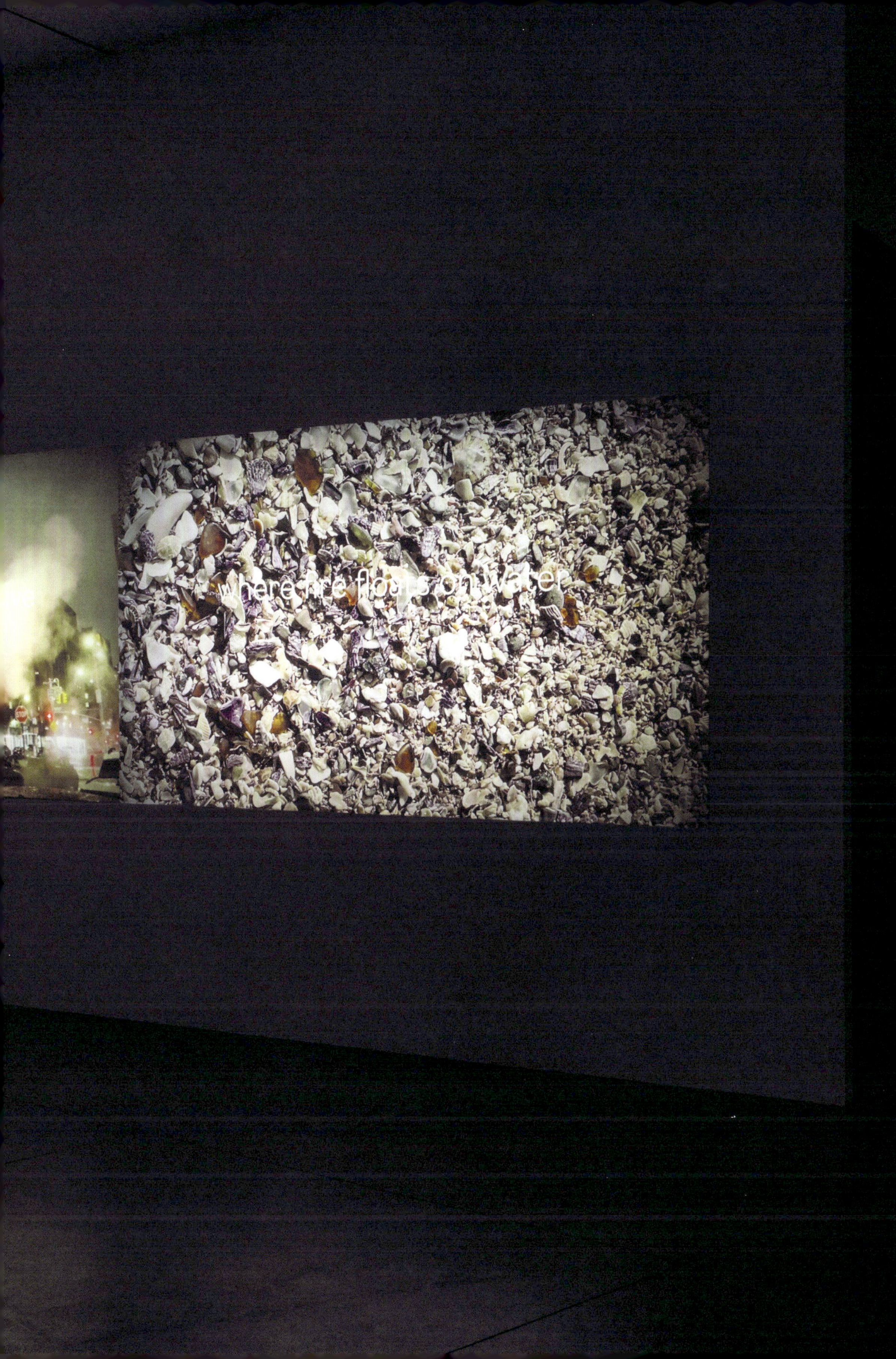
where fire floats on water

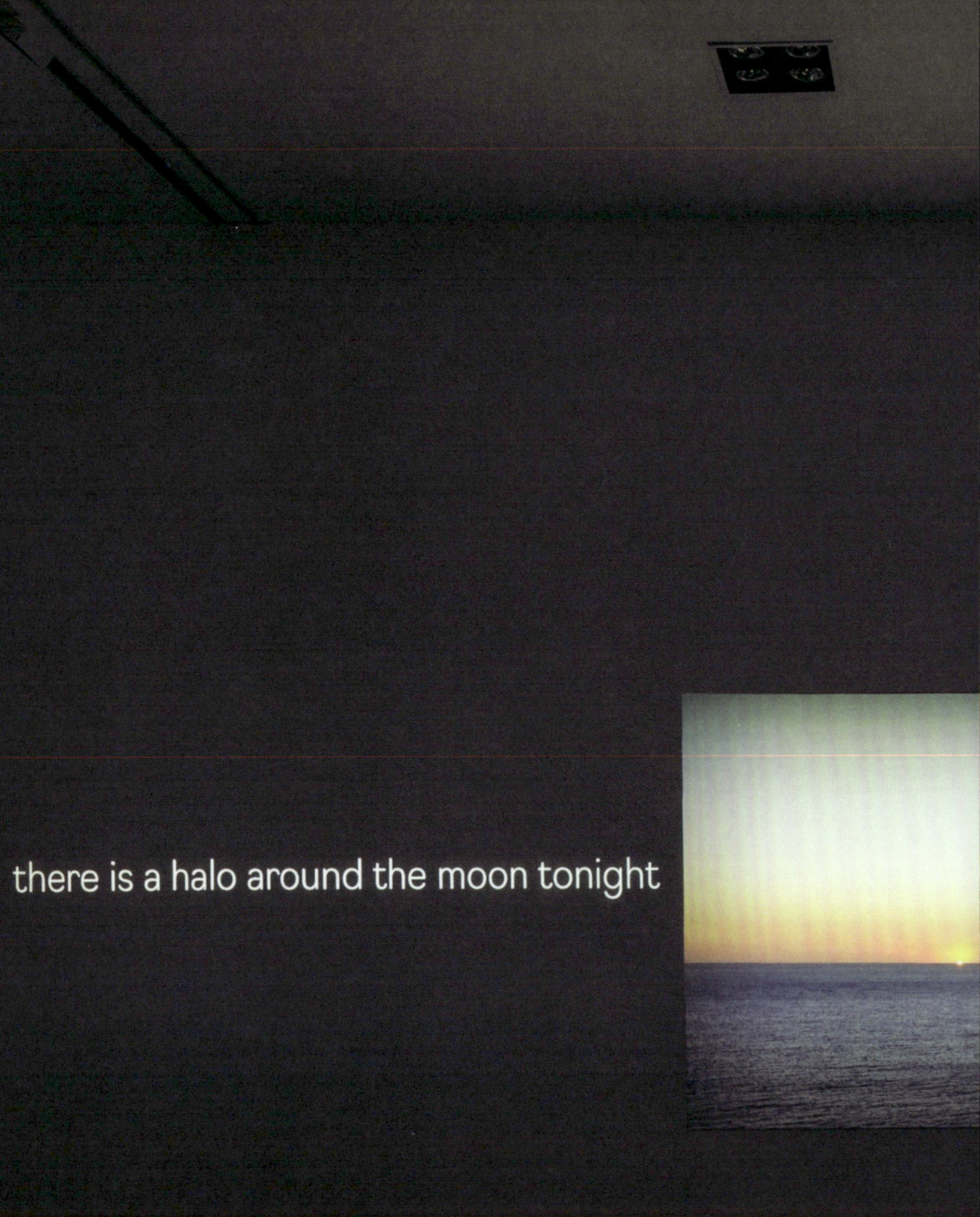
there is a halo around the moon tonight

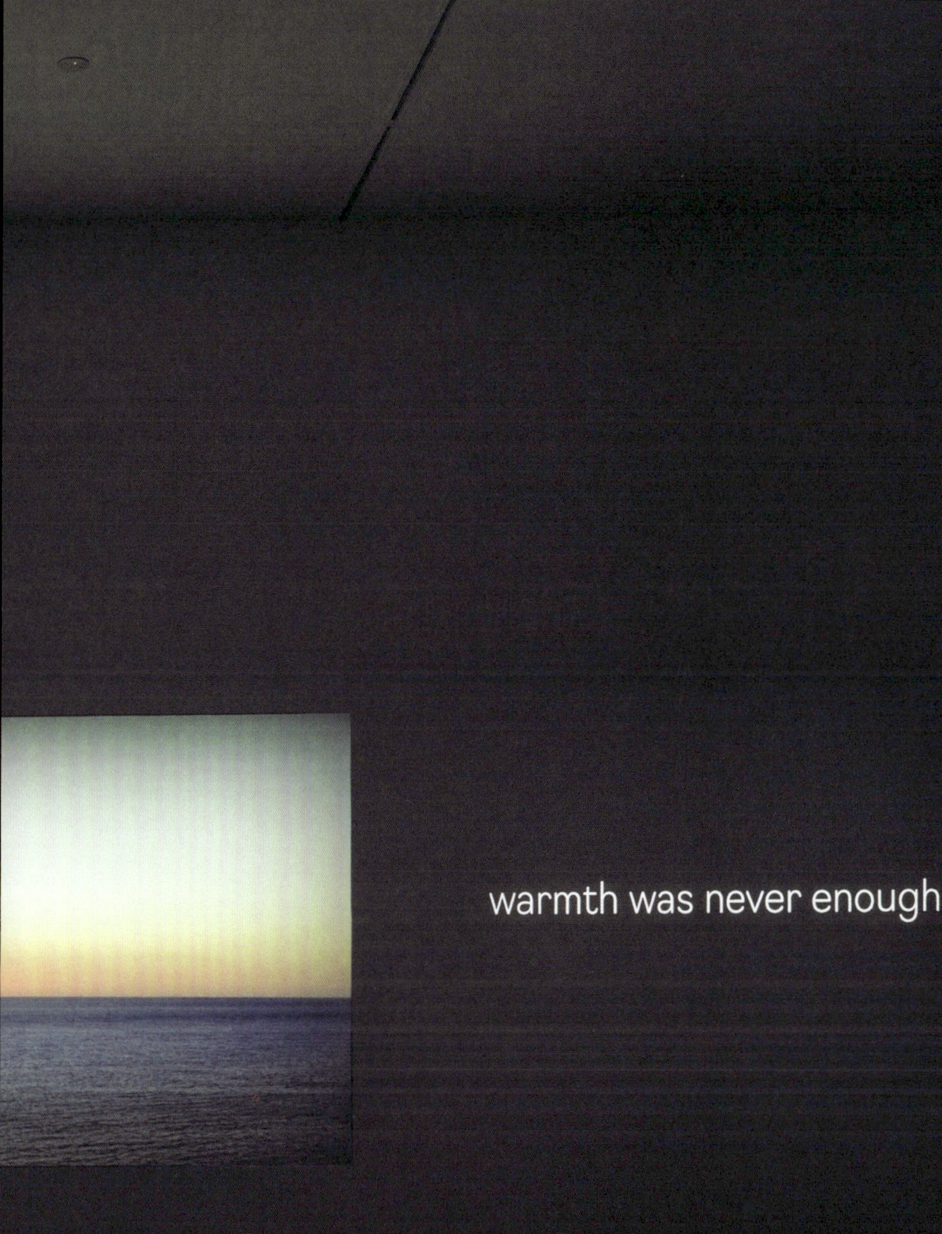
warmth was never enough

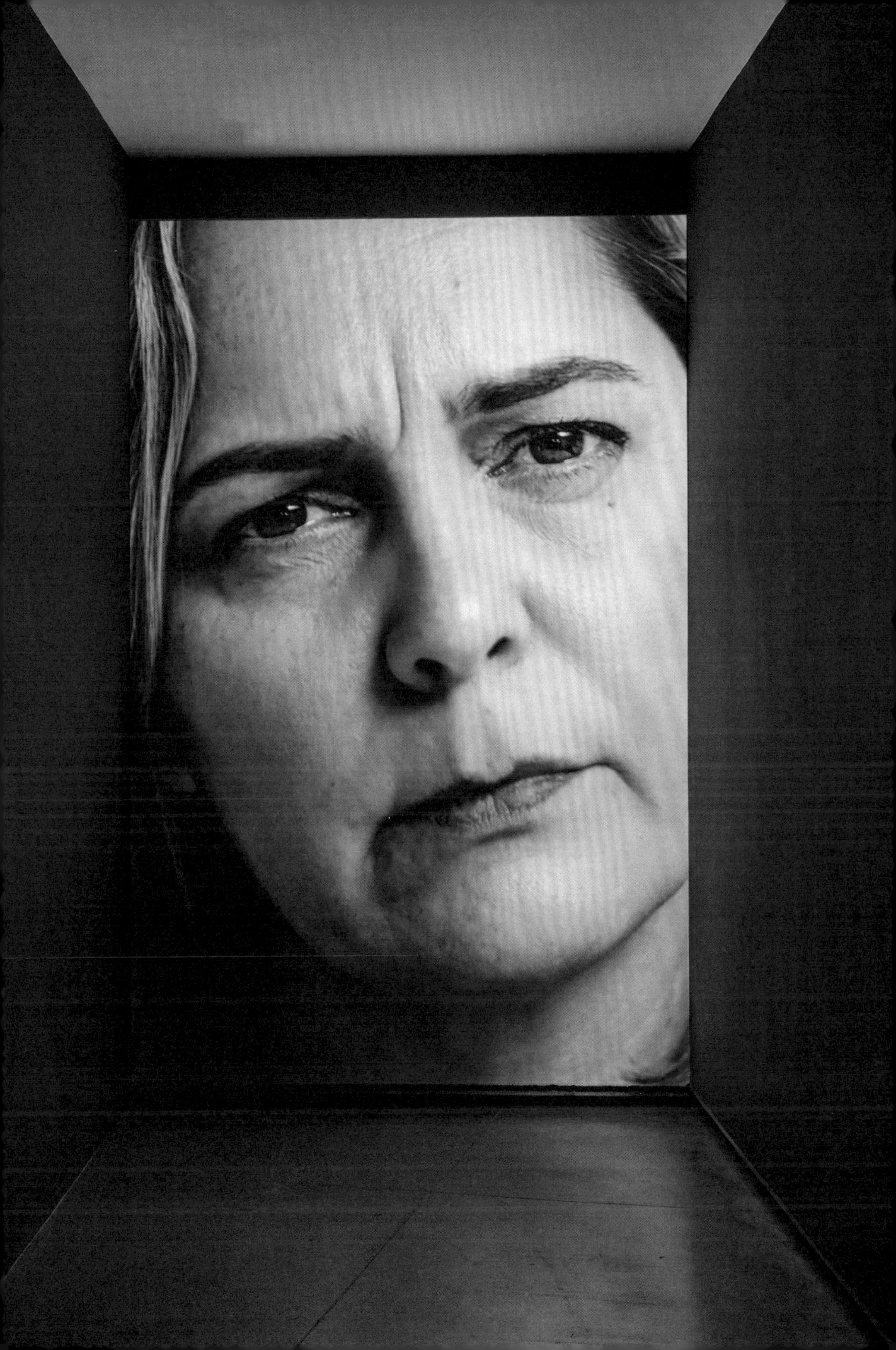

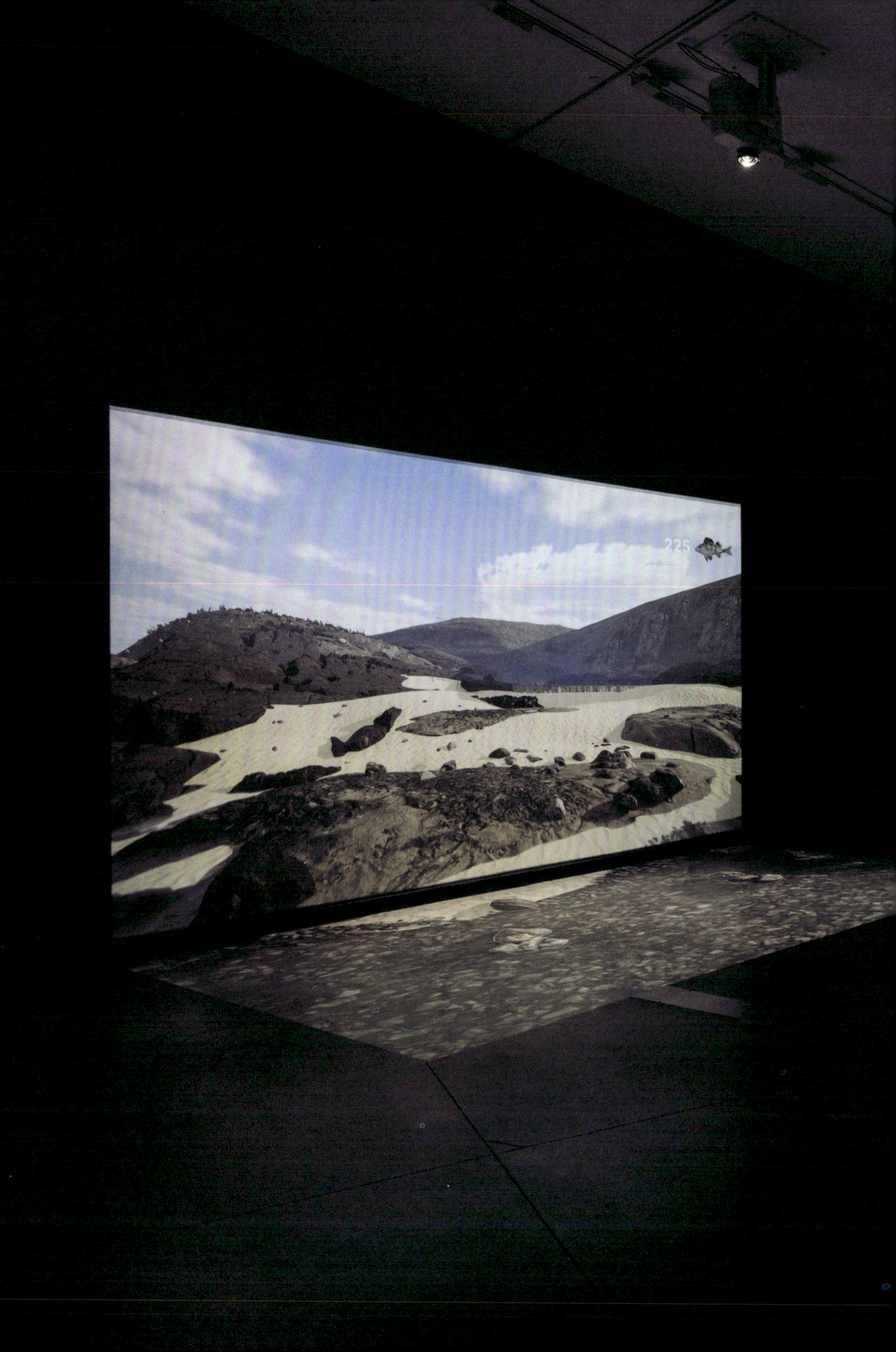
225

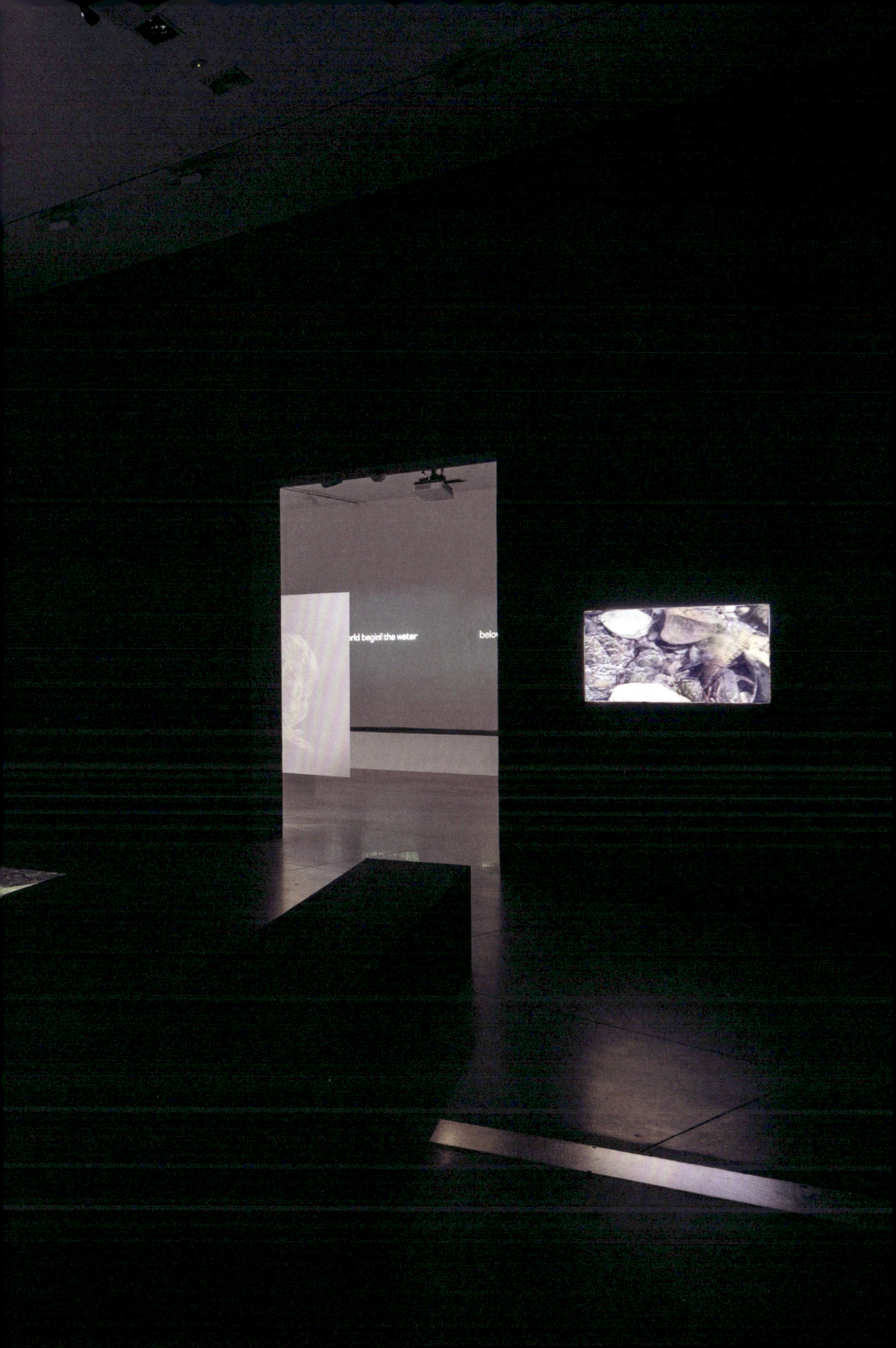

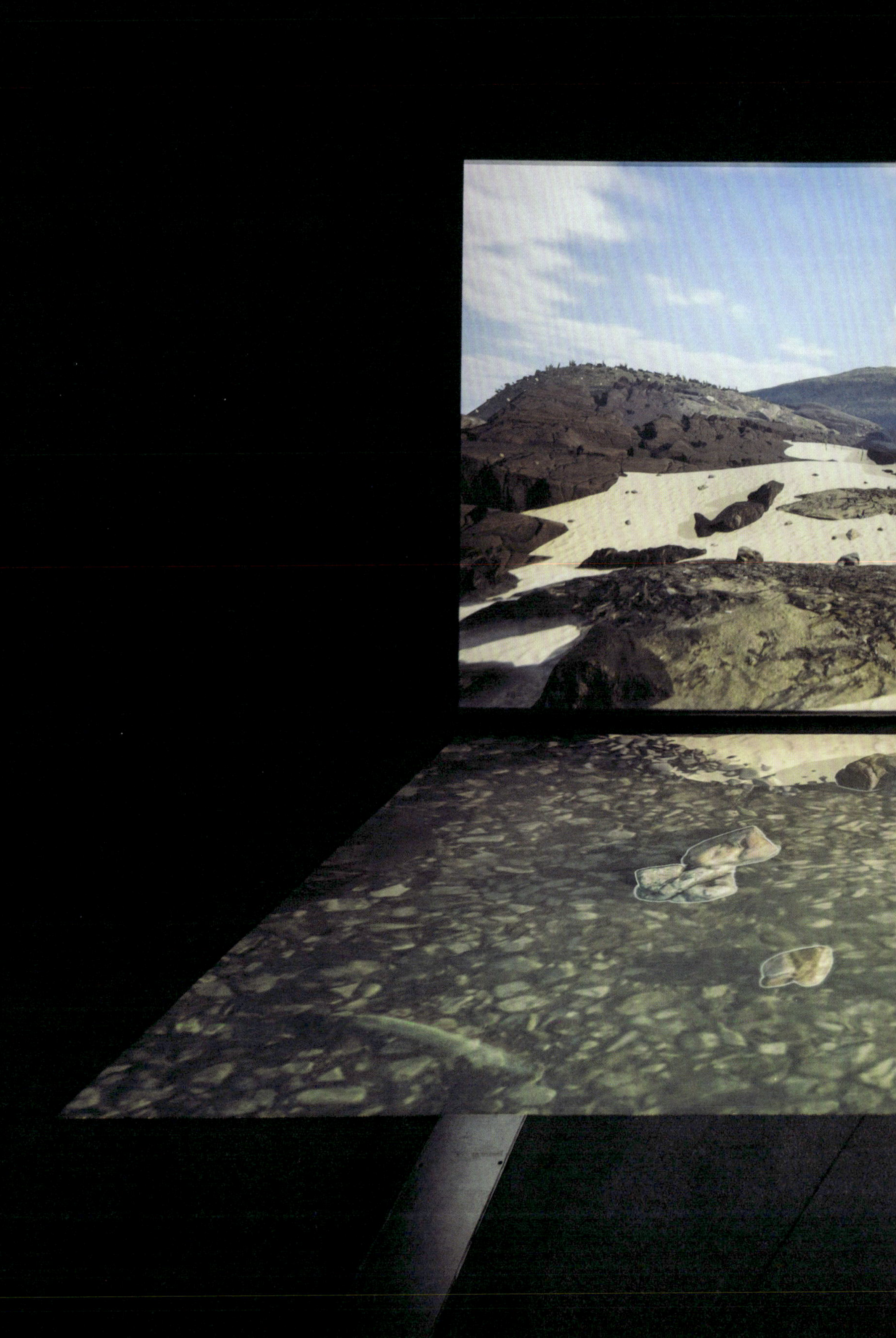

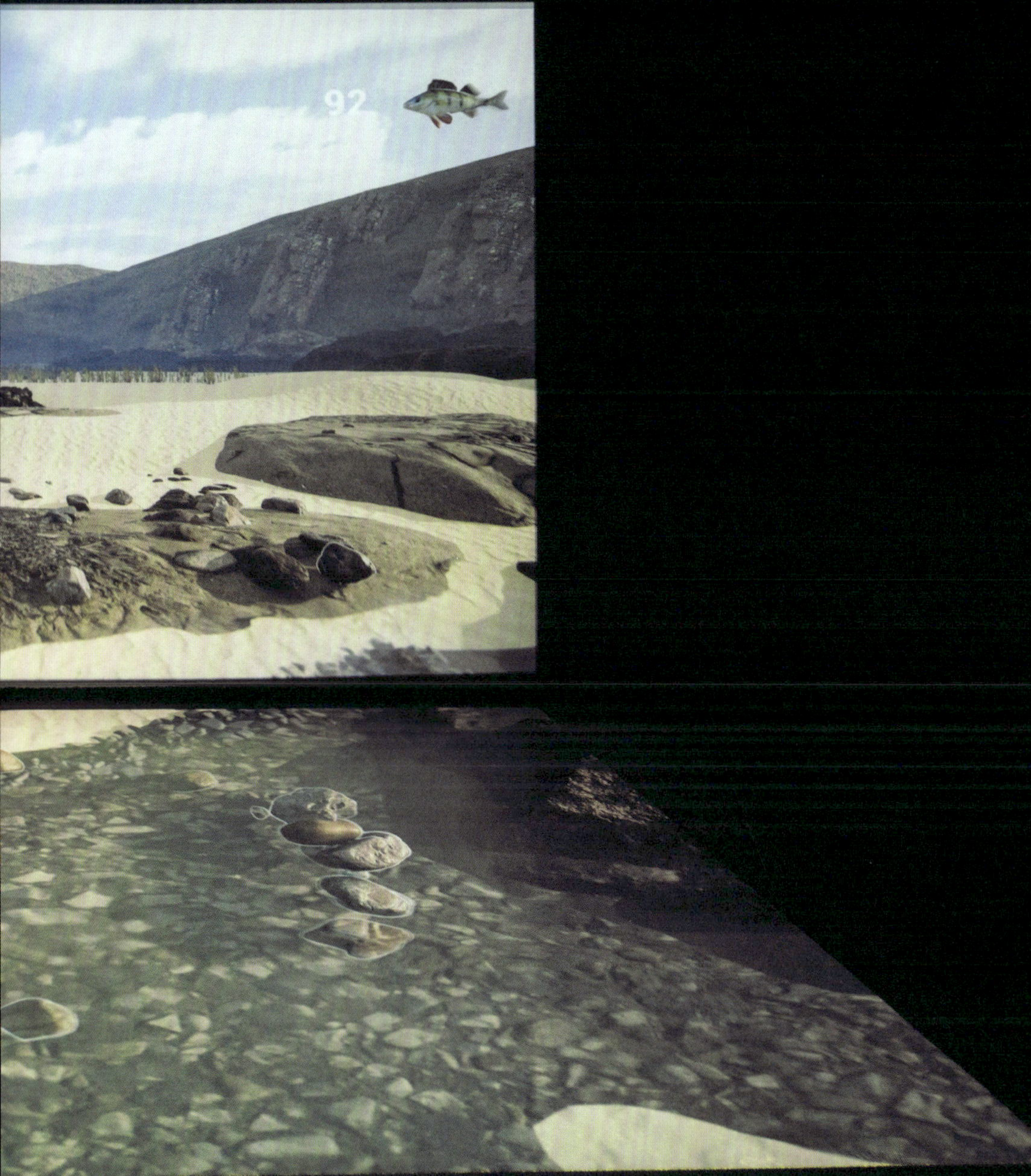
92

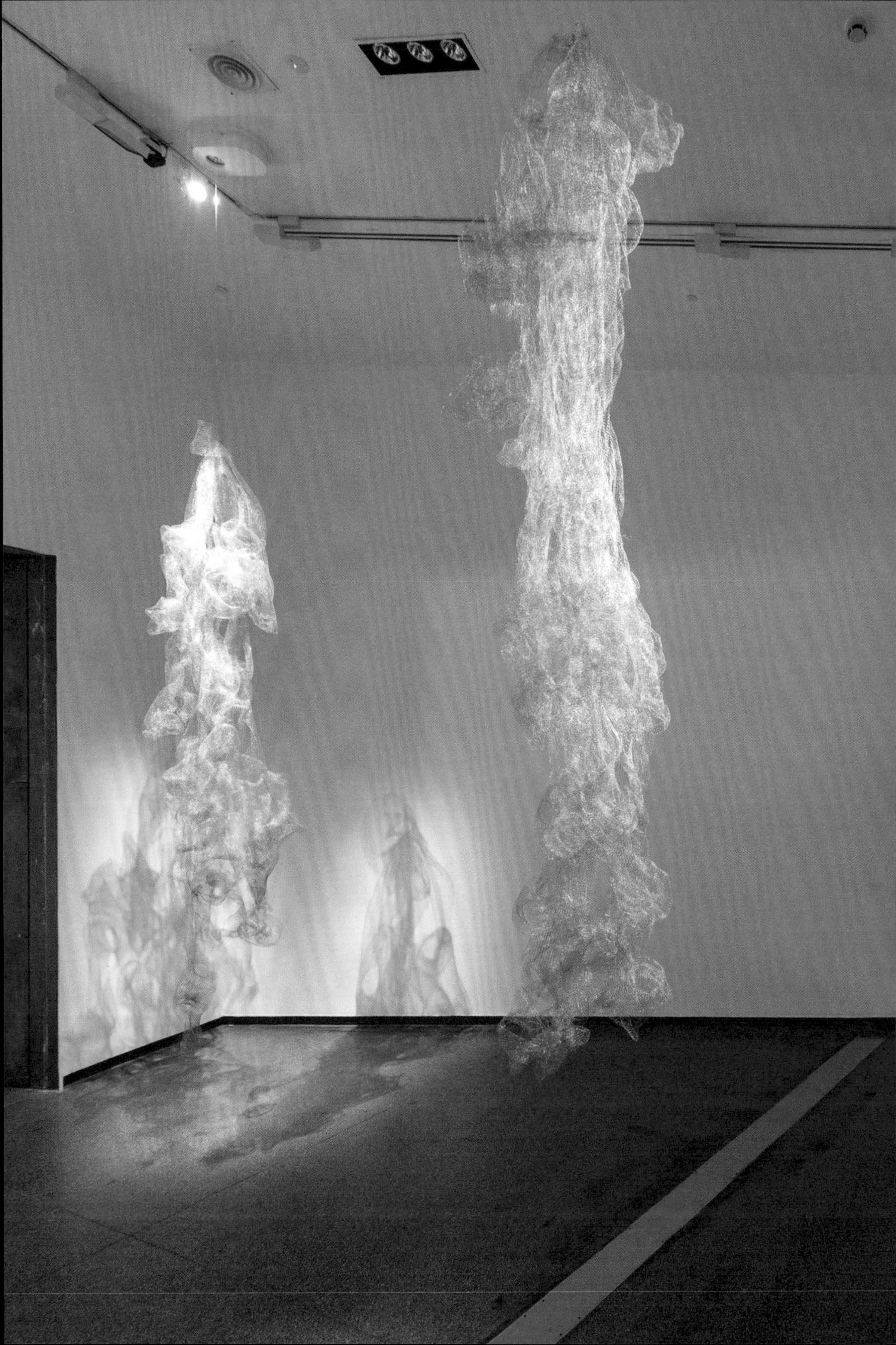

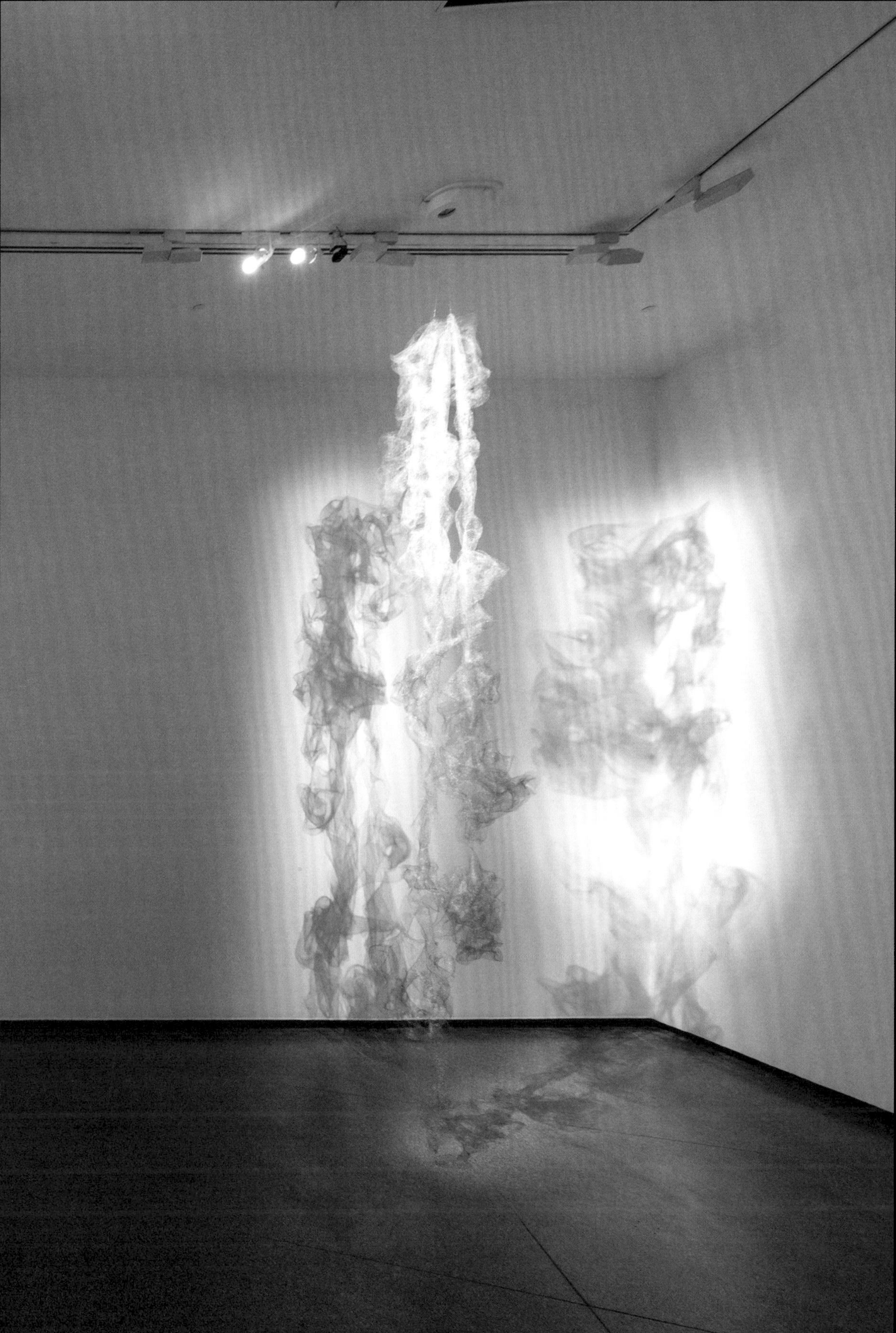

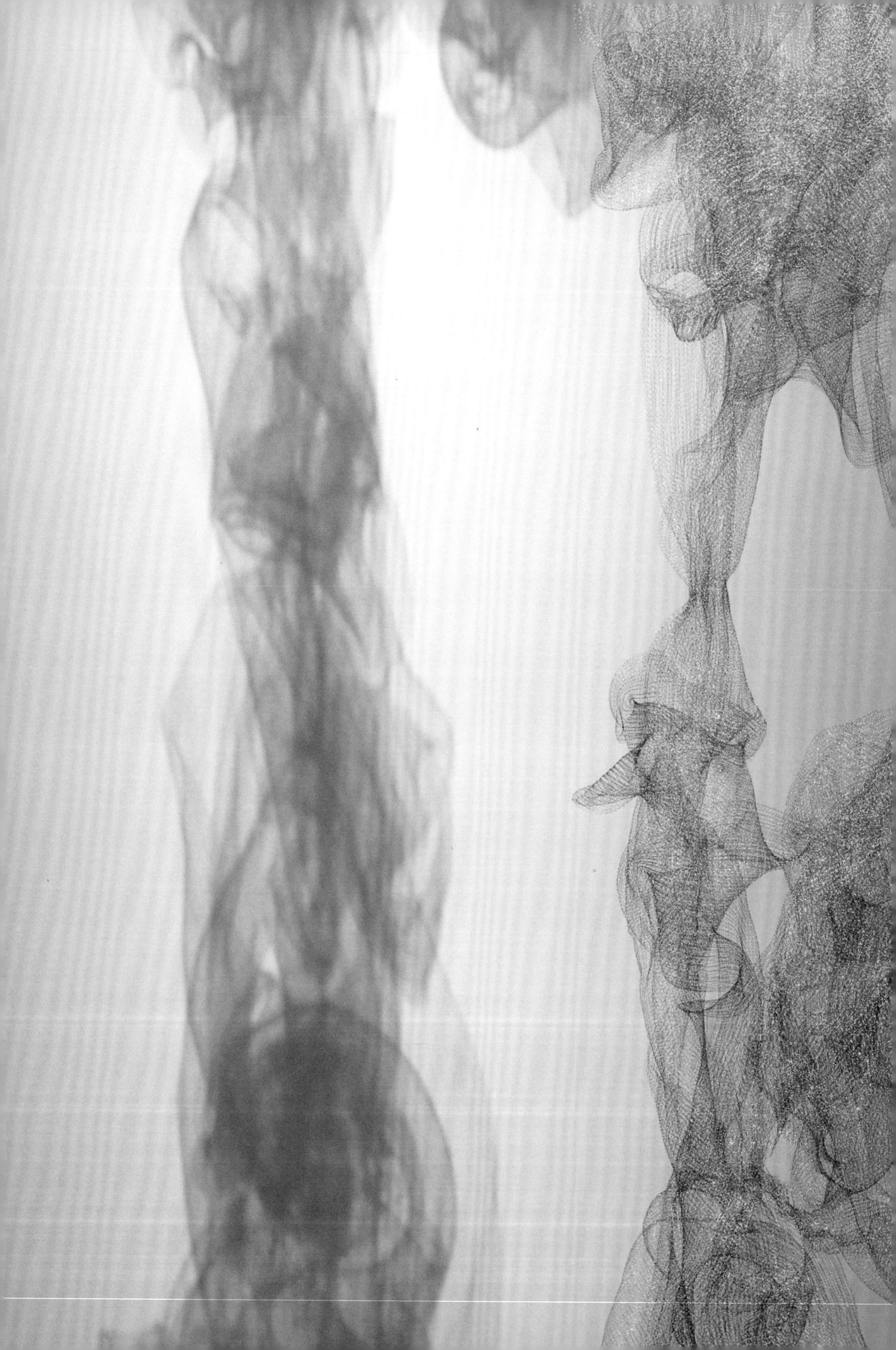

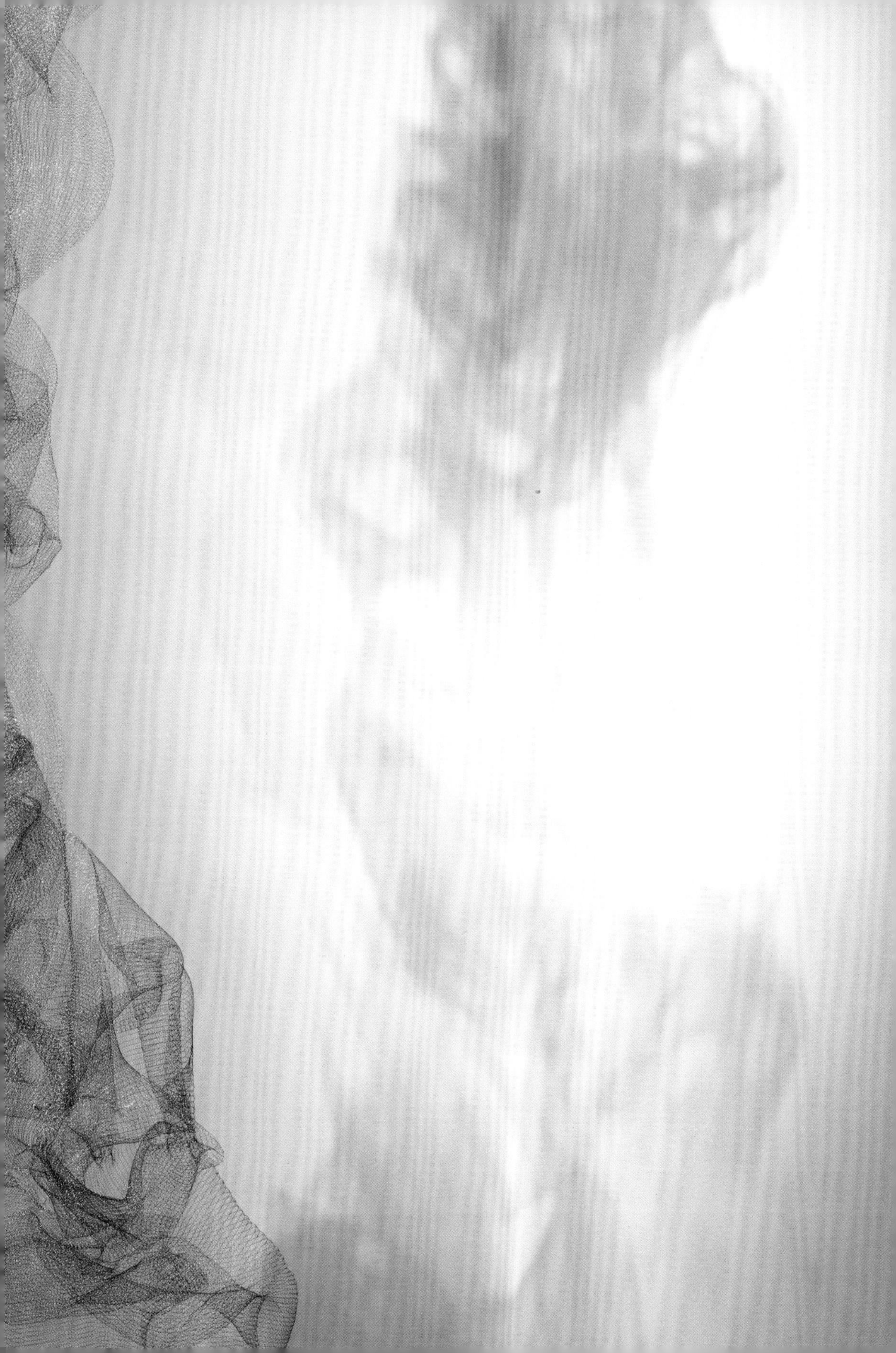

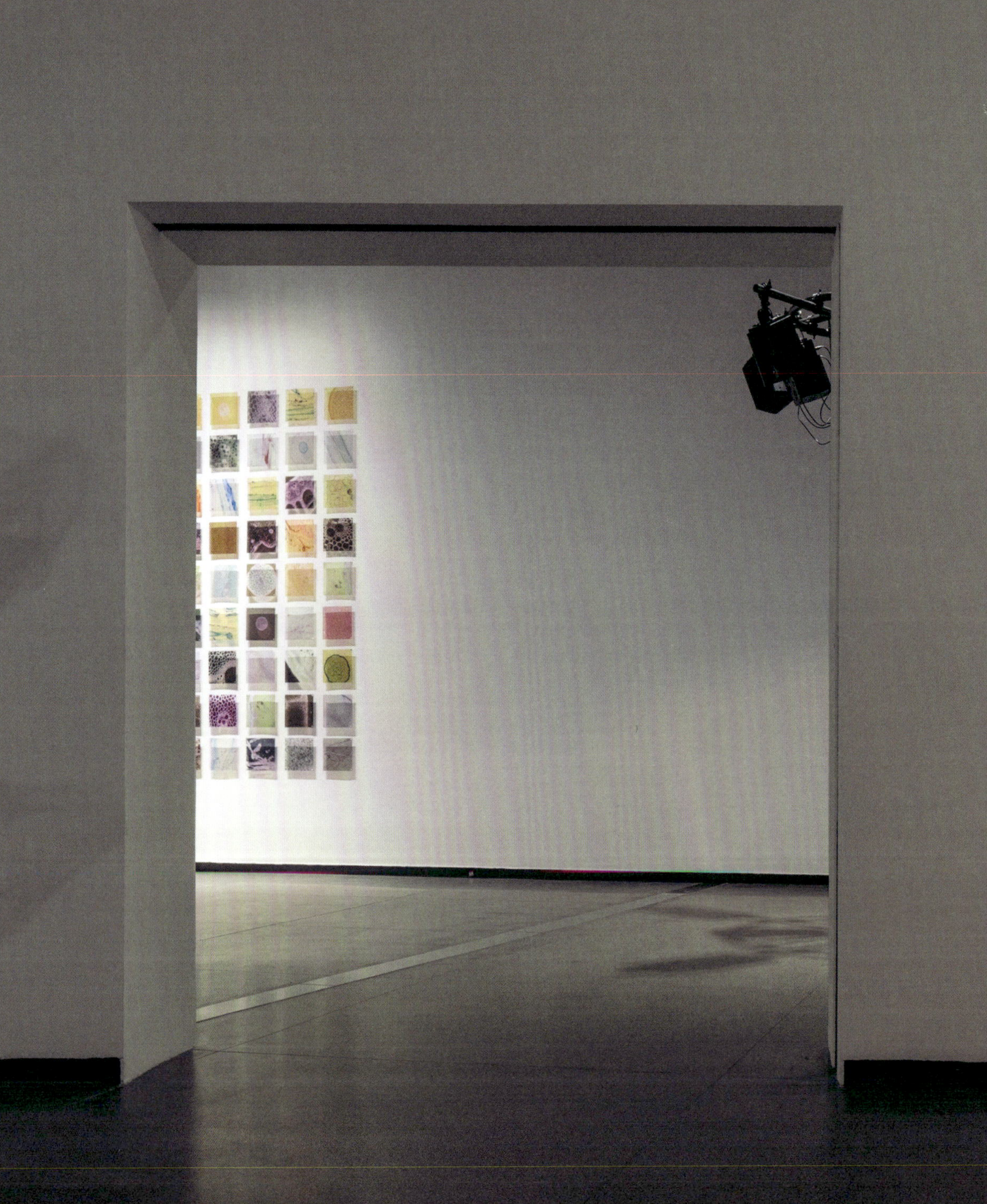

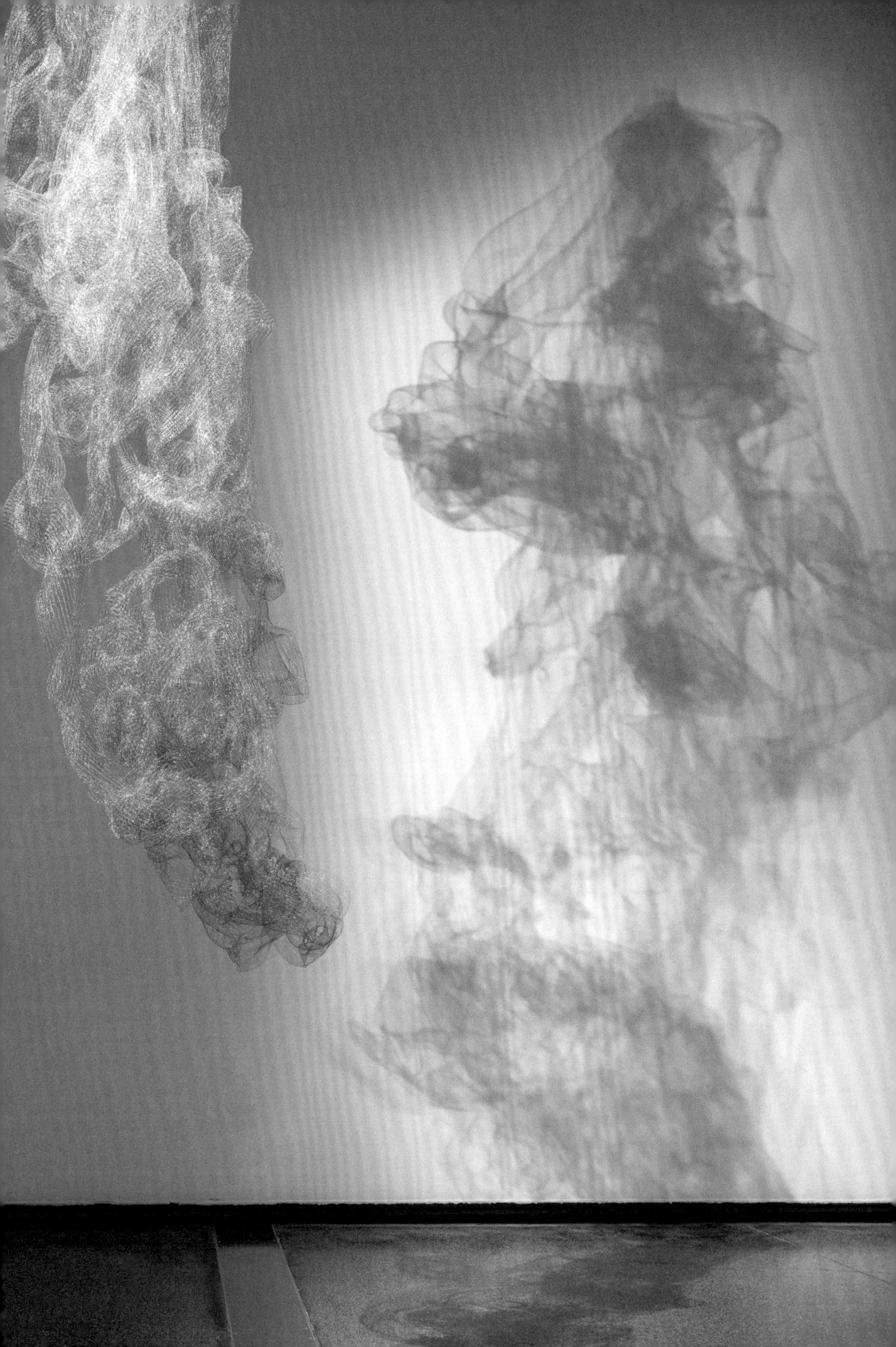

Installation Views

18-21 James Howard, *Subterranean frequencies* 2023, installation view
22-25 Maree Clarke, *now you see me: seeing the invisible #1* 2023, installation view
26-29 *Between Waves*, installation view
30-33 Dean Cross, *On who goes to The Gallows* 1997-2023, installation view
34-37 Matthew Harris, *Consigned to oblivion* 2023, installation view
38-39 *Between Waves*, installation view
40-41 Cassie Sullivan, *wayi (to hear)* 2023, installation view
42-45 Jazz Money, *infinite iterative piece* 2023, installation view
46-47 Hayley Millar Baker, *Entr'acte* 2023, installation view
48-49 *Between Waves*, installation view
50-51 Brad Darkson, *waiting for kakirra* 2023, installation view
52-55 Mandy Quadrio, *Not gone!* 2023, installation view
56-57 *Between Waves*, installation view

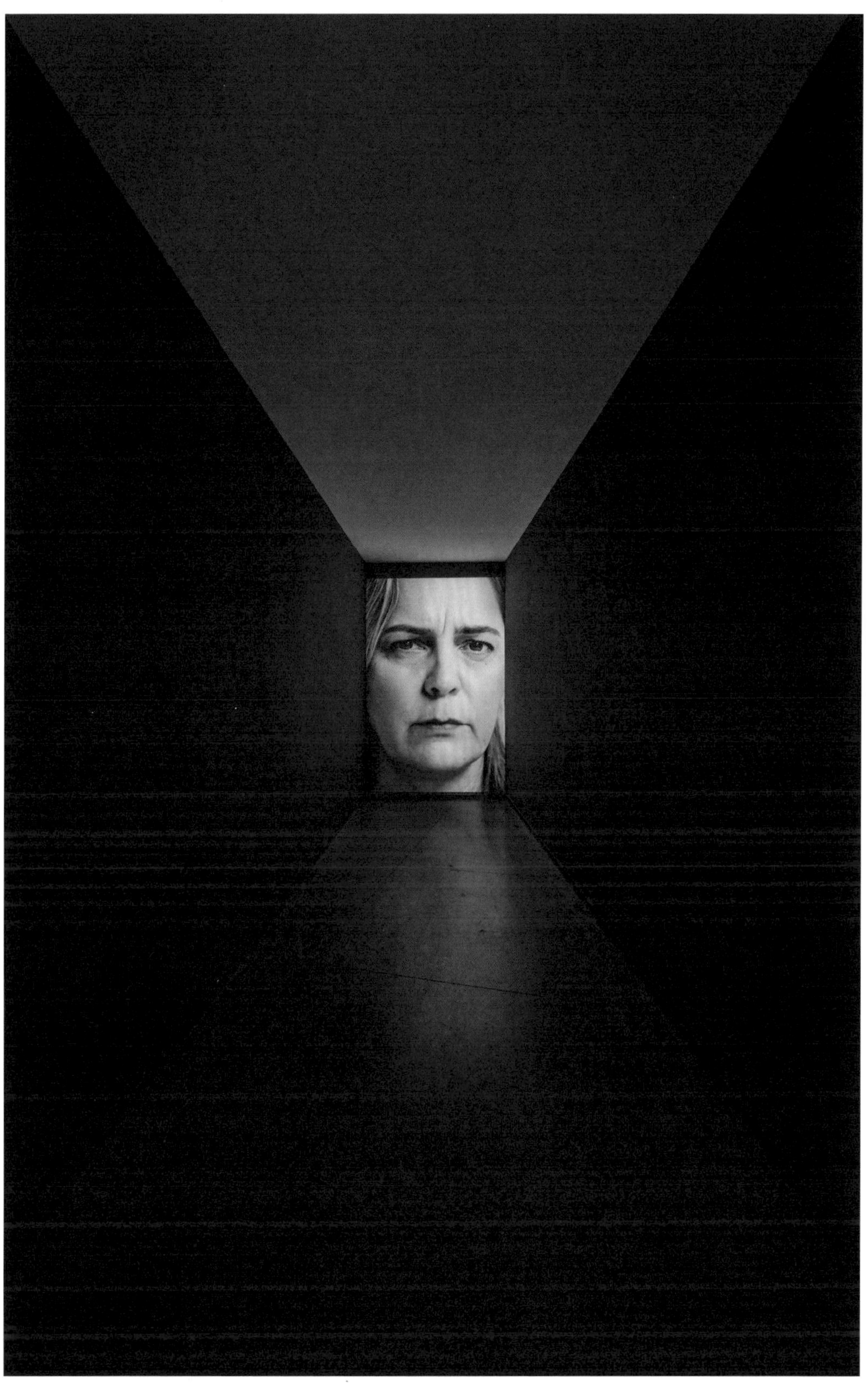

Hayley Millar Baker, *Entr'acte* 2023, installation view

Blood-Memory Cultural-Flows
Natalie Harkin

Kumarangk | remember a small island peaceful and slow where the fresh and salt waters meet. a ferry used to cross these waters. pelicans take a free ride to stand wise and proud waiting for fish and dreams to catch — until that bridge. how sad the people who cannot slow down to ride with a pelican. lower lakes churn memory toward her wide-open mouth so we taste blood and bone resting deep and shallow while casuarinas sigh sing and cry up the wind. reeds push through her silty skin to be picked and dried and soaked to weave precious stories of Old Ones. from fish traps to midden sites her sand dunes drift-settle-shift and rest so everywhere a trace of her on tides — from birth-life-death to birth. all past-present-futures pump from the land our brown body. this small island. they said she fabricated her beliefs but we know there is no horizon to the stars and her seven sisters will never end. we will know her fight for justice and ngatjis and babies and ancestors for as long as it takes. as long as it takes for a small island. Ngarrindjeri yarluwar-ruwe. known by some as Hindmarsh Island. always Kumarangk. these cultural flows.

Charlotte | every Saturday morning the Tuckwell boys walk a familiar route along the river's edge for fish to buy. the best catch in the district they say. scaled-trimmed-gutted and honoured with care. they cut through town to trace a slight rise behind Armfield Slip and stop just before reaching the railway line. Walker's Camp. they call it the outskirts but Old Nanna Charlotte calls it her beating heart. the last semi-traditional people in Goolwa they say. respected and proud. renowned fishers and weavers and fighters in white wars. her pulgi is rough with iron sheets and hessian bags on a spread of thorny weeds. inside is beautiful and clean. neat as a pin. come midweek she delivers her catch across town before landing herself on Old Lady Tuckwell's deep verandah. they drink hot tea from bone china. she smokes her pipe. the young Tuckwell boys see her as a grumpy old woman. a mystery pungent with river-gifts. it's 1936 and she is eighty-five years witnessing. she knows colossal invasion and colonial-entitlement as dangerous and deep as the river is wide. townsfolk with pitchforks hunger for prime-land while she sleeps. on the quiet chill of the darkest new moon her camp covertly torched one winter's night. horror flames. impossible to contain. Old Nanna Charlotte fades as river-sorrows churn and rise to meet her plight. her blood-memory streams toward that canoe tree place where she finally rests so we remember. from womb to womb and the force of time see her glow with the moon to shimmer blackened tides. these cultural flows.

Karra | slow agitations occupy tributaries with dredging and fracking and South-East drains. concrete networks channel fresh flood-plain waters out to sea. we are drought-stricken storm-beaten and flooded with grief. salt-crystals rise with ignorance while domestic taps run putrid in shades of cloudy-to-black. 'Public Notice Boil Water Alerts' are stapled to country town trees: *Water used for drinking or food preparation should be brought to a rolling boil to make it safe. Children should take bottled water or cool boiled water to school* (Walgett, New South Wales); *Children must avoid swallowing water or getting water up their nose when showering, bathing or playing with water* (Oodnadatta, South Australia); *Boiling the* [arsenic-poisoned] *town water will not make it safe to drink and bottled water should be used for drinking, food preparation, making ice, cleaning teeth and gargling* (Uralla, New South Wales). our sacred Country under siege might best be conjured from the perspective of fish. small spotted and swift or giant Elders of the deep. they glide strong and quiet. carve rivers as stories and stories as rivers to feed and glisten and spawn new life. blue-green algae fully thrive to bloom then die. oxygen levels fall and asphyxiation levels rise. Karra. Old River Red Gums carrying centuries of story lean in to witness. fish thrash wildly at her roots then chase stagnant shallows toward a slow gentle float. they rest in their millions as layers of riverbank sediment transform to hot dried clay. these mighty trees bearing floodwater stains recognise massacre and drop another limb with the weight of despair. as lifelines give way to a thirsty greedy chain of water-thieving infrastructure our Elders seek reflections of home and weep. they demand — 'who will honour the fish?'. these cultural flows.

Yartapuulti | small at the wharf's edge. face west across the water to see a $2 billion redevelopment all lit up in neon satisfaction. this high-rise high-density waterside housing for the rich. this glittering neo-colonial backdrop reflected on her black night's river. face west across the water to this potent site. Lartelare's birthplace and remnants of home. she is *keeper of the black swans.* Yartapuulti. this river flooded with story carries memory on undercurrents that pull and twist in surprising directions. moments are captured and dragged down to settle with sediment. seep into past-present-future memory. imprint on fine silted skin. this translucent familiar is like a drop of essence. a spill of blood. a lingering trace as black-swan ripples hold our gaze. as the river swells dive in to drink it all then dissolve on time luring deep-deeper toward shards of light that slice and glide. a soft sliding fade where sun cannot reach. where surfaces no longer glisten. this is the quietest-dark and never still. search for memories on currents and decades of protest. find flags flying peace and torrent-rage. generations of bloodshed and tears drive the tides to open-up to taste it all. sweet solidarity reflects new neon-light-stories on a dark moon and we are still awake in the land of sleep. we are still afloat on the land of grief. here at this site we remember. we miss our beloved elder-Aunty-wise friend. Aunty Veronica. this float of imaginings flows straight to her heart and together we watch *campfires lit up all the way to Outer Harbor… just like fairyland.* no high-rise-neon-light-dreams here. only Lefevre-Peninsula-Love on a quiet drift. these cultural flows.

Cultural flows | we are mangrove and rock hole and fresh water spring. we are mighty drifts of brown-green-blue to seep and drain from vein to outlet to river and sea. we rest with midden sites and blue whale bones and sandy ridges and chenier plains. we find memories of old ways interrupted and sit with Elders who know how to stay awake in this land of sleep. we are inherited responsibility so future generations will know this once-upon-a-time perfectly balanced magnificent web of life. they will know to hold space for lands-waters-spirits-skies. they will know to carry culture and lore and epic beauty forward as whole and fragmented and vibrant and disrupted. we are ocean life spawning in seagrass blankets. we are tidal marshlands labouring hard to ebb-flow and lure fish and crabs and snails to creeks at high and low tide. these flows can't be calculated by suits and assessment tools in scientific spreadsheets but are lived and loved between waves of story and blood-memory-honouring. like salt-of-the-earth we rise to settle-unsettle survive and thrive and we refuse to disappear. these cultural flows.

Between realms of memory and materiality

Tina Baum

From the beginning of time the First Peoples of ~~Australia~~[1] have lived along the coastlines and inland waterways where the rhythmic waves of water washed along the shoreline carry nourishing and life sustaining food. The cyclical light of sunrise, sunset, the night skies and fire have also lit and guided countless peoples across landscape and waters. Country holds the Ancestors and spirits between realms, with culture embedded in the land, waters and sky.

These life sustaining elements have connected people to their homelands, to their Communities and their culture for millennia. The artistic and cultural expression of Indigenous people have always been evident in the landscape if you know where to look: from rock art and engravings, to carved trees and stone formations. Indigenous artistic expression in all its forms – art, dance, song, and now moving image and writing – conveys and reinforces artists' identity, which evolves over time through collective experience and individual innovation. It's this continuity through time, space and place that connects and informs Indigenous people today.

From 1770 onwards, however, these same salty waters also floated in outsiders and catastrophic change, with waves of Aboriginal smoke signals rising along the east coast warning others of their presence. Starting at ground zero, the initial clash between the Gweagal people of the Eora Nation and the British at Kamay/~~Botany Bay~~, was rapidly followed by frontier wars and waves of disease, death and destruction, as colonisation rippled across the continent forcing dispossession and displacement that shattered cultural life.

First Nations art and culture was also collected, stolen, plundered, destroyed, appropriated, and ironically used as identity icons for the newly formed ~~Australia~~. Despite this, nineteenth century artists like Wurundjeri-balluk artist William Barak (1824-1903) and Kwatkwat Tommy McRae (c.1835-1901) had thankfully documented and drawn ceremonial life from memory and experience, and recorded visions of colonisation in ~~Victoria~~. Dhurga artist Mickey of Ulladulla (1820-1891) from ~~New South Wales~~ also documented local flora and fauna and Larrakia artist Billiamook Gapal from the ~~Northern Territory~~ had his drawings of ceremonial dancers and food sources shown in Naarm/~~Melbourne~~ at the 1888 Intercolonial Exhibition, albeit as 'primitive art'. This event showed Naarm as one of the earliest cities in ~~Australia~~ to officially feature Aboriginal art. These early artworks continue to provide important counter narratives and invaluable perspectives and reference points for many Aboriginal artists and Communities today.

For the Wurundjeri Woi-wurrung, Boon Wurrung and Bunurong peoples of the South-Eastern Kulin Nation of Naarm/~~Melbourne,~~ their waves of change started before colonial establishment in 1835. Now, other off Country Indigenous artists who live in Naarm have formed new connections to people and place.[2] For the nine artists and one collective featured in *Between Waves* their established and new connections are crucial to their experiences and memories of place. Their works and stories are interlinked through a collective First Nations memory and through acts of reclamation using new technologies and innovative ways of creating and engaging cultural knowledge.

For senior Yorta Yorta/Wamba Wamba/Mutti Mutti/Boonwurrung artist Maree Clarke, the reclamation and revival of cultural practice taken and made dormant since colonisation is central to her practice. Known for her visionary life-sized possum skin cloaks, kangaroo tooth necklaces or up-scaled *Phragmites australis/*river reed necklaces, her innovative culturally informed contemporary practice also includes photography and moving image. Maree's newly commissioned work explores the microscopic internal and external structures of *Phragmites australis*. The use of light and coloured dyes to penetrate the thin cross sections of cell walls, exposes the organic structures and unique patterns within, revealing the cellular in between spaces that still hold Country and memory. Her ambitious photographic projections highlight the visible and invisible, and the interrelationship between light, sound and material memory as part of her collaboration with The University of Melbourne Histology Platform. The interrogation of this organic material normally used in traditional necklaces creates a continuity of the old and new combining culture and science that advances her arts practice to new levels.

Worimi artist Dean Cross cleverly juxtaposes memory through the physical representation of photos, letters, objects and paintings he has collected and carried with him since birth. The evocation of emotion, connection and memory through these items tell a very personal story and journey. He asks, 'are we the sum of all our experiences? Or are we somehow something more?' Does the collection of things provoke important memories or does it represent identity through life's physicality and experiences, through archives and stories? Traditionally events and information were told and retold through oral stories and through the memory and meaning of objects over time. Dean, growing up off his Country, re-positions his connection in new places, family and identity through his work.

Aboriginal cultural presence in the landscape is everywhere. For ~~South Australian~~ Narungga artist Brad Darkson his work, featuring a traditional stone fish trap, typically located in a riverbed, waterways or ocean shoreline, is moved into the white cube gallery and digitally represented through interactive photogrammetry software. By encouraging audiences to engage through physical interaction, the work creates movement in the three-dimensional plane. This active engagement temporarily arranges the digital stones before they realign to their original position. By combining tradition with new technology and encouraging active audience engagement, Brad highlights ongoing cultural conservation and restoration practices used by his Community.

Yorta Yorta artist Matthew Harris's works feature a re-creation of seven large-scale minimalist paintings featuring museum archival shelves. Using ochre, he has painted 'stacked' archival boxes on each shelf giving a view of standard museum storage. These shelves reflect the centuries-long museological practice to collect, study and exhibit Indigenous Ancestral Remains, cultural and restricted objects and art. Museums contain many dark secrets and have a problematic history with Indigenous peoples. Matthew aims to interrogate these gate-keeping institutions and to shed a light on this history through his work.

For Jaadwa artist James Howard his sound sculpture installation elicits emotion through the hidden vibration of sound. His audio field recordings, gathered from invisible and visible sites around and under ACCA's building, amplify the embedded sounds of Country. His asynchronously layered sonic response to deep sounds remind audiences of the eternal earthly presence of Aboriginal culture. Often overlooked, audio works are an important inclusion in the exhibition, challenging the hierarchy of other senses, and privileging their conectedness.

Aboriginal people have been recorded, photographed and filmed extensively by colonist authorities. As an act of reclamation and repositioning, Gunditjmara artist Hayley Millar Baker has created a new video work focussing on internally restrained rage and grief expressed through a singular female protagonist. Titled *Entr'acte* – referring to an interlude performed between two acts of a play – the work provides a voyeuristic view of the relentless and inequitable emotional, spiritual and mental weight women are forced to carry and contain, often socially restricted from release. Simultaneously light and dark, hidden and revealed, the work exposes the emotional focus, determination, strength and power intensely projected in this intimate portrait.

As a writer and poet, Wiradjuri artist Jazz Money has created an immersive three-channel video work that expands her unused personal archive of writings and 'lost lines', presented in unrestrained and arbitrary configurations. The known text is indiscriminately revealed in unknown and infinite arrangements reflecting the random and ever relentless information accessible to humanity and the constant desire for total understanding. In its unpredictable arrangements, the work becomes a poetic 'exquisite corpse' as fragments of text are juxtaposed to create an ever changing composition.

Visions and memories of Country are diffused across palawa artist Cassie Sullivan's large-scale monoprints on clouded acrylic sheets. They are reminiscent of a thick mist that floats across her Country in lutruwita/trouwerner (~~Tasmania~~). The works create a maze that audiences navigate, as they view imprints of cloth that Cassie has dragged and pushed with her body over land and water at sites of significance on melukerdee and nuenonne Country. The cloth captures and reflects the physicality and bodily memory of action, also the capturing of Country and the generational memory that accompanies it, enabling the creation of new memories for her.

The blak arts collective *this mob* have created an exciting interactive digital zine by core members Yorta Yorta/Wurundjeri/Wiradjuri artist Moorina Bonini, Taungurung artist and writer Kate ten Buuren, Gulumerridjin(Larrakia)/

Wardaman/Karajarri artist Jenna Lee, Luritja artist Jenna Rain Warwick, and Lardil/Yangkaal emerging writer and curator Maya Hodge. Their new digital commission features an array of creative and cultural works of photography, poetic texts, recorded yarns, mini feature films, interviews, recipes, gardening tips, crossword puzzles, and more. Together, *this mob* weave conversations, experiences, and memories that unfold through a considered process of deep listening and collective making, to map connections and disconnections with one another, the self, and the world.

Trawlwoolway and Laremairemener artist Mandy Quadrio sublimely uses netted steel and wire mesh fabric to respond to the buried and hidden colonial histories in lutruwita (~~Tasmania~~). Her twisted metal forms look like smoke slowly billowing up, much like the warning signals about colonial outsiders. The forms also recall x-rayed landscapes with undulating hills and valleys as the metallic mesh moves and transforms, perhaps hinting at or revealing the hidden histories of her Tebrakunna, ~~Cape Portland~~ homelands. Her steel wire forms aim to undo historic denials and imposed Aboriginal invisibility, with Mandy's weaving of metal and use of light creating shadows across the installation space – in doing so, she scours away the injustices and weaves Aboriginal perspectives back into the historical narrative of ~~Australia~~.

For Southeast Indigenous artists living and working on or off Country they continue to tell and reveal personal experiences and collective memories, all importantly from Aboriginal perspectives. Naarm held the earliest showcasing of works by Aboriginal artists and this continues today with the Yalingwa exhibition series at ACCA. For many Aboriginal and Torres Strait Islander artists who continue to live on Country, and for those who live off Country, the memory of, or desire to, stay connected to culture, Community and Country remains strong. For many living in the Southeast they still tell the stories hidden and known, reclaiming, and repositioning their original versions of history.

The powerful curation and artworks in *Between Waves* nod to the first waves of incursion between insiders and outsiders along the Southeast of ~~Australia~~, whilst elevating the artists' voice and hidden stories. The exhibition showcases and reinforces the dynamic excellence of Southeast Aboriginal art. It shows the ongoing presence of Indigenous people in place, across time and between space. Importantly the exhibition honours the Wurundjeri Woi Wurrung word 'Yalingwa', *shining a light on the times*, by bearing witness to truths.

For palawa/pallawah curator Jessica Clark, the third curator in the Yalingwa initiative, she has drawn together these incredible emerging and established artists to present their newly commissioned video, installation, poetry, projection, sculpture, sound, and performance works that respond to identity, site, sight, sound, space and time. Jessica's multidisciplinary framework for the exhibition also explores the cyclic and sensory rhythms of light, time, and vision. The memory held in each work also adds to the collective memory of place at ACCA. She has proudly repositioned each artist within the context of Naarm/~~Melbourne~~, on Wurundjeri Woiwurrung Country, to create alternative narratives and memories that illuminate a better understanding of the multiplicity of First Nations identities in the Southeast.

Between Waves is part of the Yalingwa Visual Arts Initiative, an invaluable curatorial opportunity for outstanding practitioners to present a major exhibition focusing on Southeast Australian First Nations artists within a national context. The initiative also provides an opportunity for a major senior Aboriginal artist living in ~~Victoria~~ to be recognised and celebrated with an Artist Fellowship. Opportunities like these are critical to elevate Indigenous presence and creative and cultural practice in place.

This major exhibition remains an important legacy to those gone before us and those with us now and those yet to come. *Between Waves* positions artists at the forefront and makes their artworks and stories visible; acting as constant reminders that we always have and always will be here, to let the art speak and shine a light on the times.

1 All words with a strikethrough denote British assigned place names before Federation and the establishment of Australia to disrupt their colonial names. See: Matt Chun and James Tylor, *The UnMonumental Style Guide*, 18 January 2023, unmonumental.substack.com/p/the-unmonumental-style-guide.

2 Off Country describes Aboriginal and Torres Strait Islander people who live away from or have never been to their traditional homelands and are not the traditional custodians for the places in which they currently live.

Maree Clarke

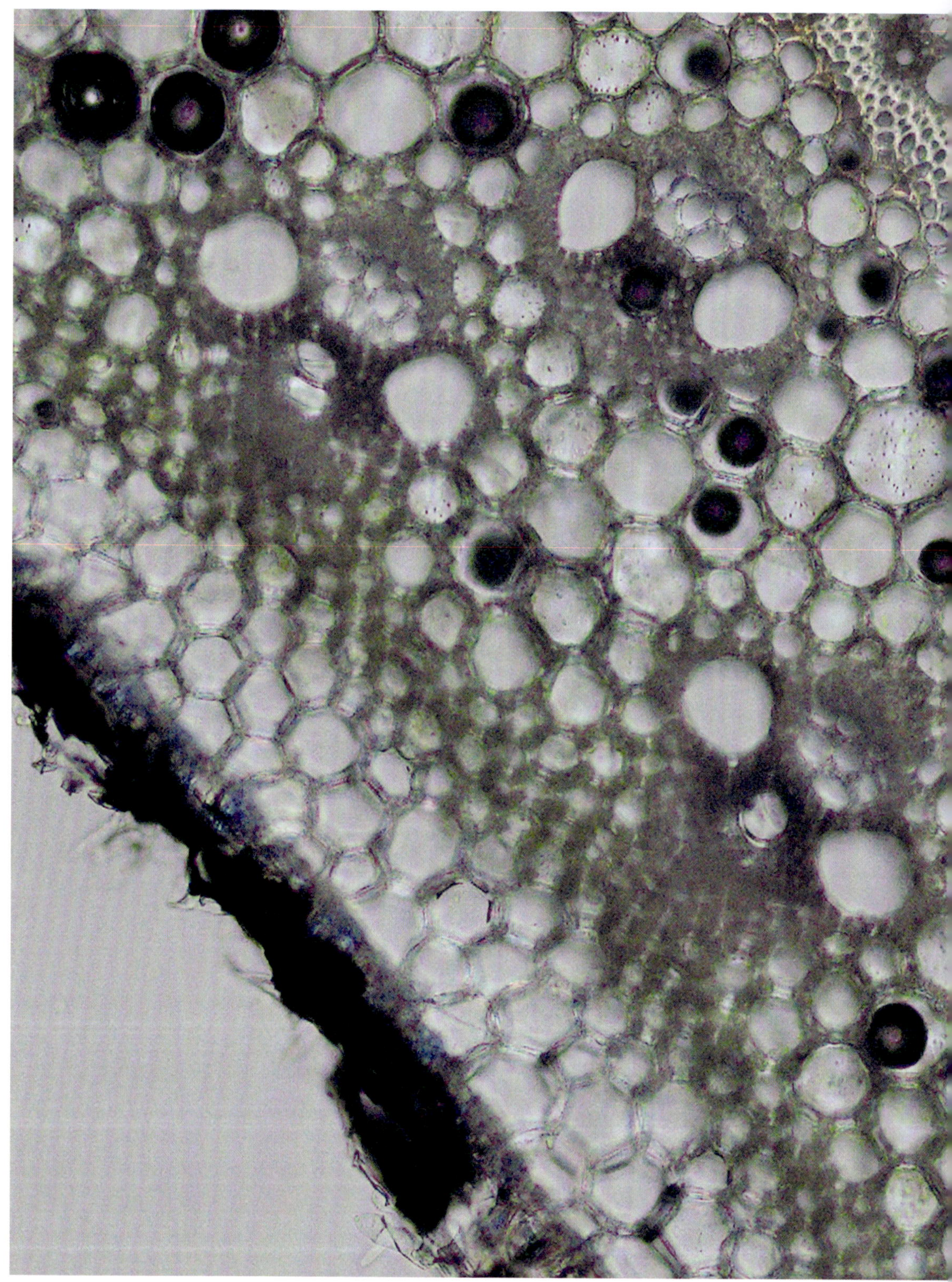

Maree Clarke, *now you see me: seeing the invisible #1* 2023 (detail)

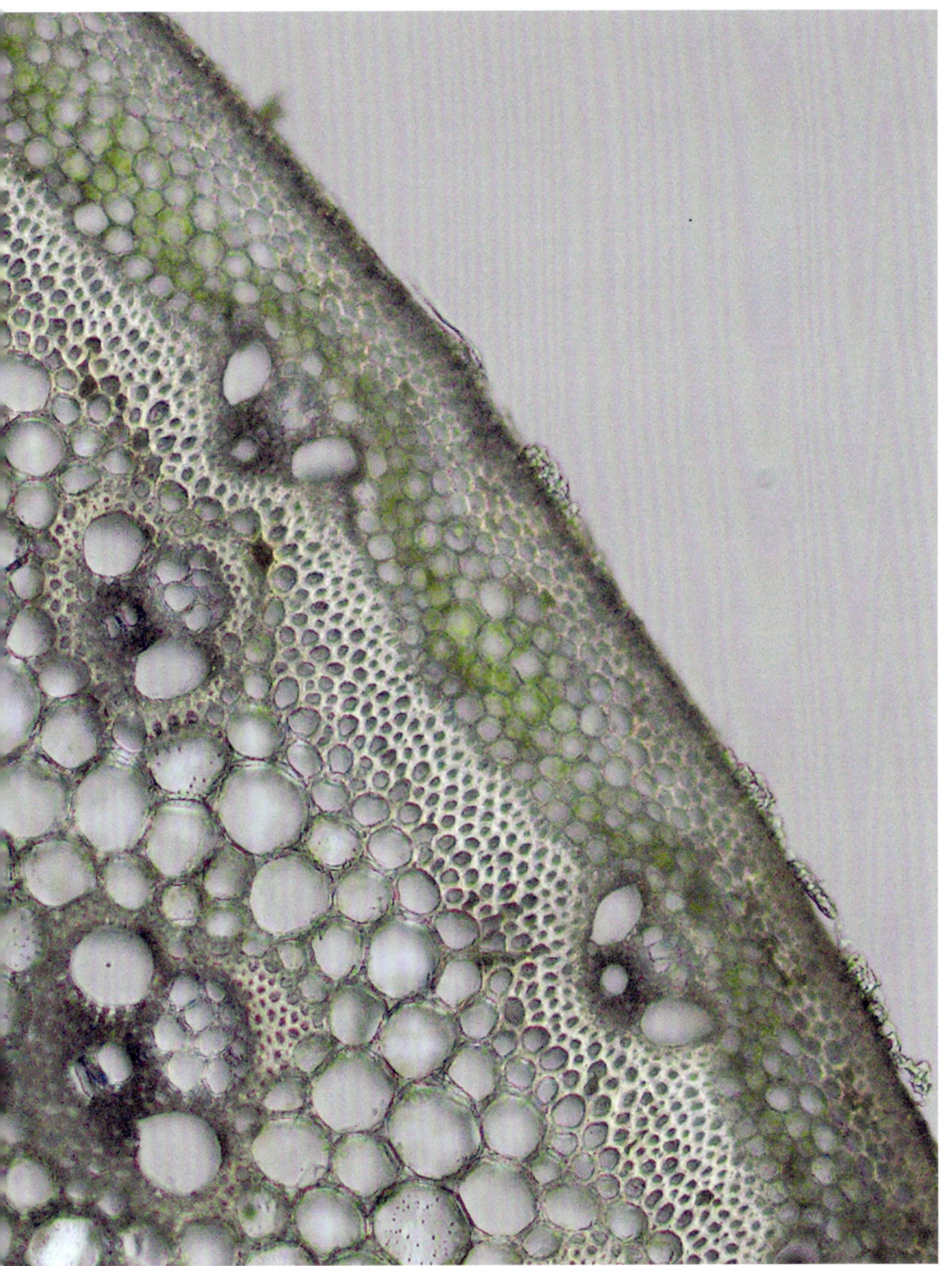

Maree Clarke

Traditionally, river reed necklaces were gifted to people passing through Country as a sign of safe passage and friendship. I have been working with river reeds since 2014, making supersized necklaces to talk about the enormous loss of land, language and cultural practices.

To do this, I have gone through a process of learning how to harvest and dye them, how to leech the salt content within the reeds to effect strong colour uptake. Through the process, the learnings and what is revealed provokes material memory, place and space.

The site where ACCA stands was once expansive wetlands that would have been filled with river reeds. For this new commission, in response to place, I started wondering about the micro systems in what is now a built environment. The ecosystems of wetland areas, seen and unseen.

Once I collected the river reeds I consulted and collaborated with the University of Melbourne's Histology Platform with Chris Freelance, Laura Leone and Paul McMillan. Histology is part of biology, the study of microscopic structure of tissues and cells for research and study. The science can identify cells, and cell structures, using microscopes. These microscopes showed the river reeds at another level altogether.

The process involves a rehydrated river reed specimen that is encased in wax, and cut by a machine, to 200th of a millimetre. It then falls into water and is picked-up by a glass slide to then view through the microscope. A camera is connected to the microscope, that is connected to the computer, and a large screen, so you can immediately see the extraordinary complexity of this micro realm.

I prepared natural specimens, and also others by adding different dyes that create a whole range of colours (such as red and blue) that I can then see interacting at a cellular level – viewing the specimen using the polariser and five different lenses (the polariser changes the colour, and the lenses change the image again). Navigating worlds through the process, zooming in and out, the slightest movement changes everything. Making the invisible, visible.

Are you a morning or a night person? Both, I love waking up early and I do tend to work into the night.

Is there a sound or song that prompts a where or when for you? Van Morrison. I like to listen to him, takes me back to the good old Mildura days.

Is there something you've always collected? I collect everything, I'm bordering on being a hoarder, but I have to be in terms of my artwork because I need different objects and items for my photoshoots. I collect lots of things, and boots, lots of boots.

Where do you feel the most connected / where do you feel the most disconnected? I really feel connected in Melbourne. I love coming back home to Melbourne and up home on Country, Mildura near the river and the desert. Disconnected not so much anywhere. I think because I love to travel so much; you just have to make your space and place when you get there and make it your own wherever you are.

What scares you the most right now / what inspires you? What scares me right now? Nothing, really. What brings me hope is, I guess, the work that I am doing and sharing knowledge with my family and community, and hopefully inspiring that next generation. Recently my great nephew has been up in Ngukkurr with his mum and dad teaching possum skin cloak making. For them to go out and do that is pretty inspiring.

Through the process of making your new commission for *Between Waves*, what has been revealed and/or become more obscured? The visibility of the river reeds and just how beautiful they are. I have loved being able to go into the Histology department at Melbourne Uni, to meet these incredible people to make this new body of work was just amazing! And for people to see just how beautiful the microscopic river reed that was revealed to me through that lens. I saw unseen worlds that look like so many different things; nebulas, weavings, eyes, seascapes, brushstrokes, cobwebs, bubbles, chicken wire, coastlines, whole galaxies and more, and that's a pretty mind-blowing experience, and one that I'm pretty excited to share with everyone.

Dean Cross

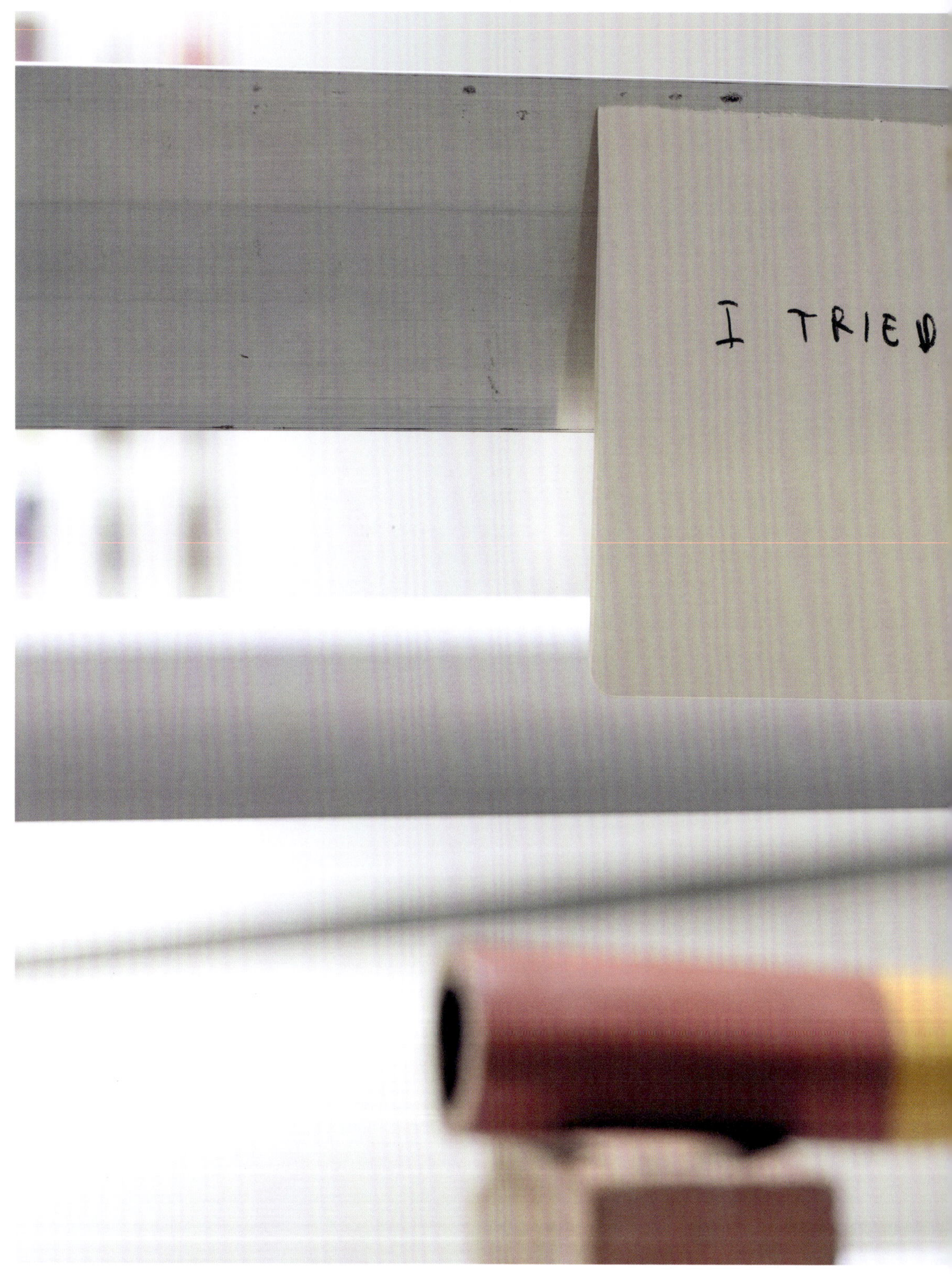

Dean Cross, *On who goes to The Gallows* 1997-2023 (detail)

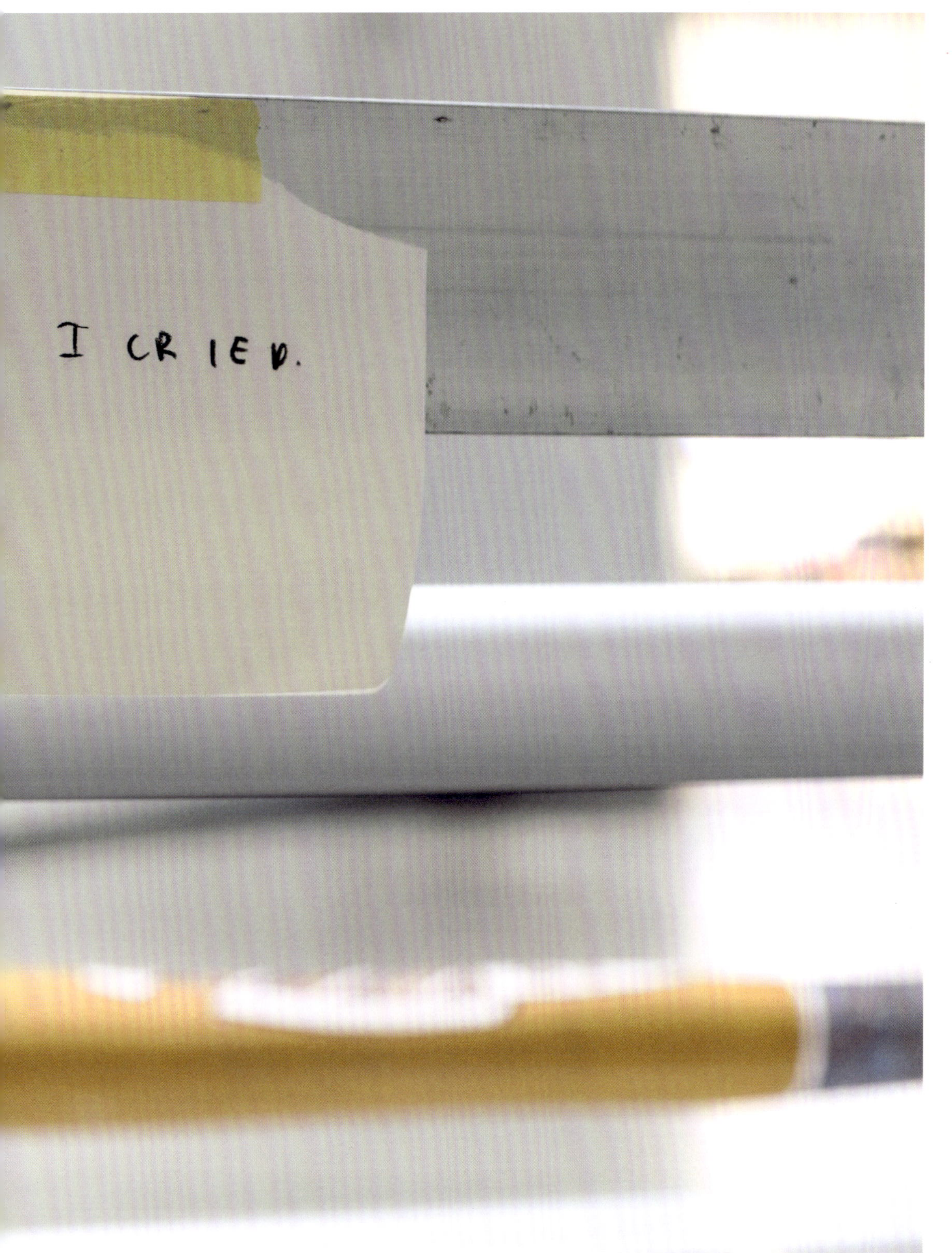
I CRIED.

Dean Cross

This is a self portrait. This is a collection of objects; a sculpture. Some of its materials have been with me since birth, others are brand new, some of its materials hold secrets, others transmit them.

I would like to tell you more, but I can't. It's too sad. I'd tell you if I trusted you or if I thought it really mattered.

And in case you are wondering, we all go to the gallows, eventually.

Are you a morning or a night person? At the moment, with four-month old twins, both.

Is there a sound or song that prompts a where or when for you? Yes, lots. Almost all of them are birds.

Is there something you've always collected? Stones, scars and books.

Where do you feel the most connected / where do you feel the most disconnected? It is the same place; the studio. But also I connect when I am fishing and disconnect when I am visiting metropolitan areas.

What scares you the most right now / what inspires you? Again, the answer is the same for both. Everything.

Through the process of making your new commission for *Between Waves*, what has been revealed and/or become more obscured? Art is life. Life is touch. Everything changes.

Brad Darkson

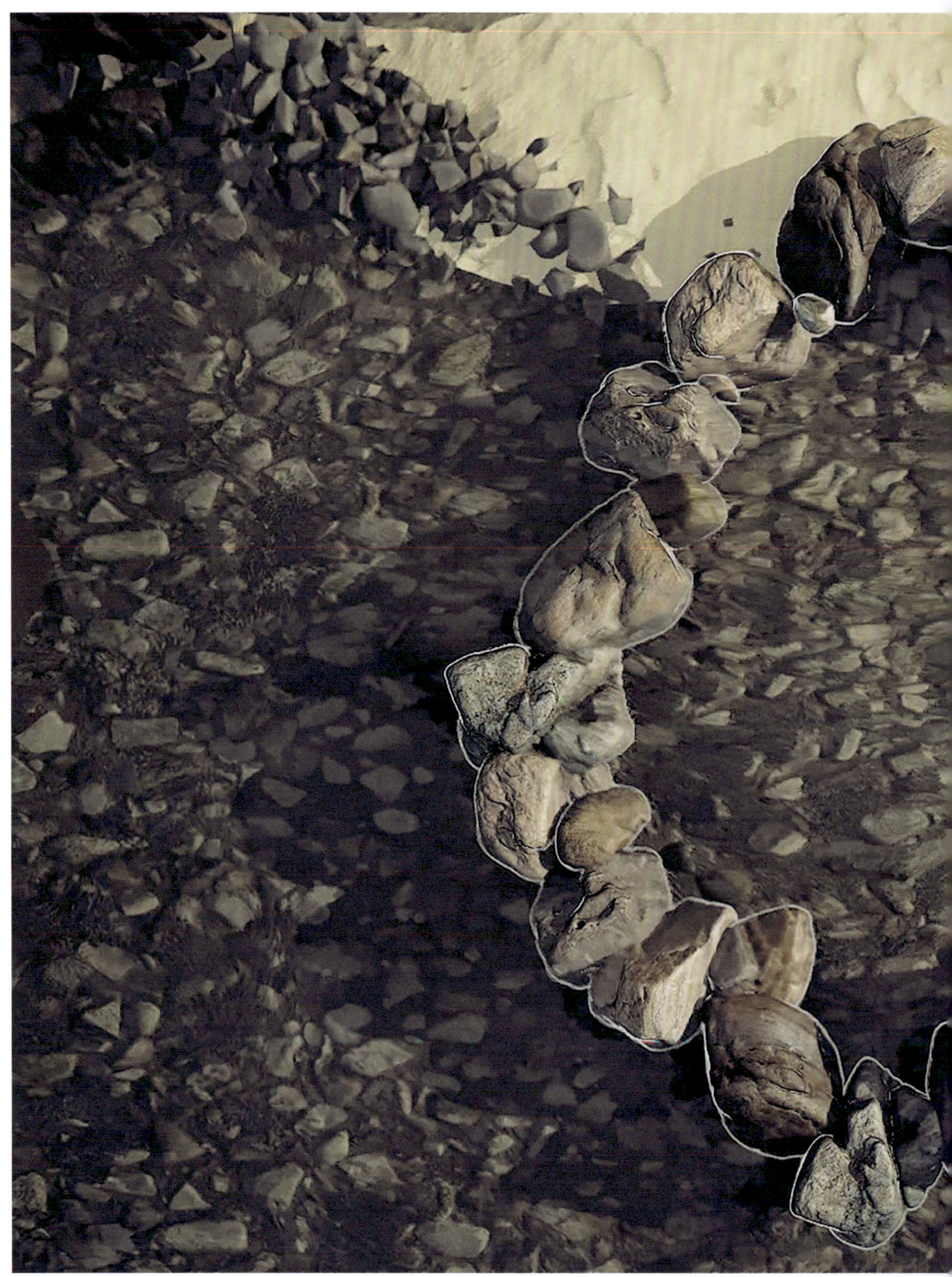

Brad Darkson, *waiting for kakirra* 2023 (detail)

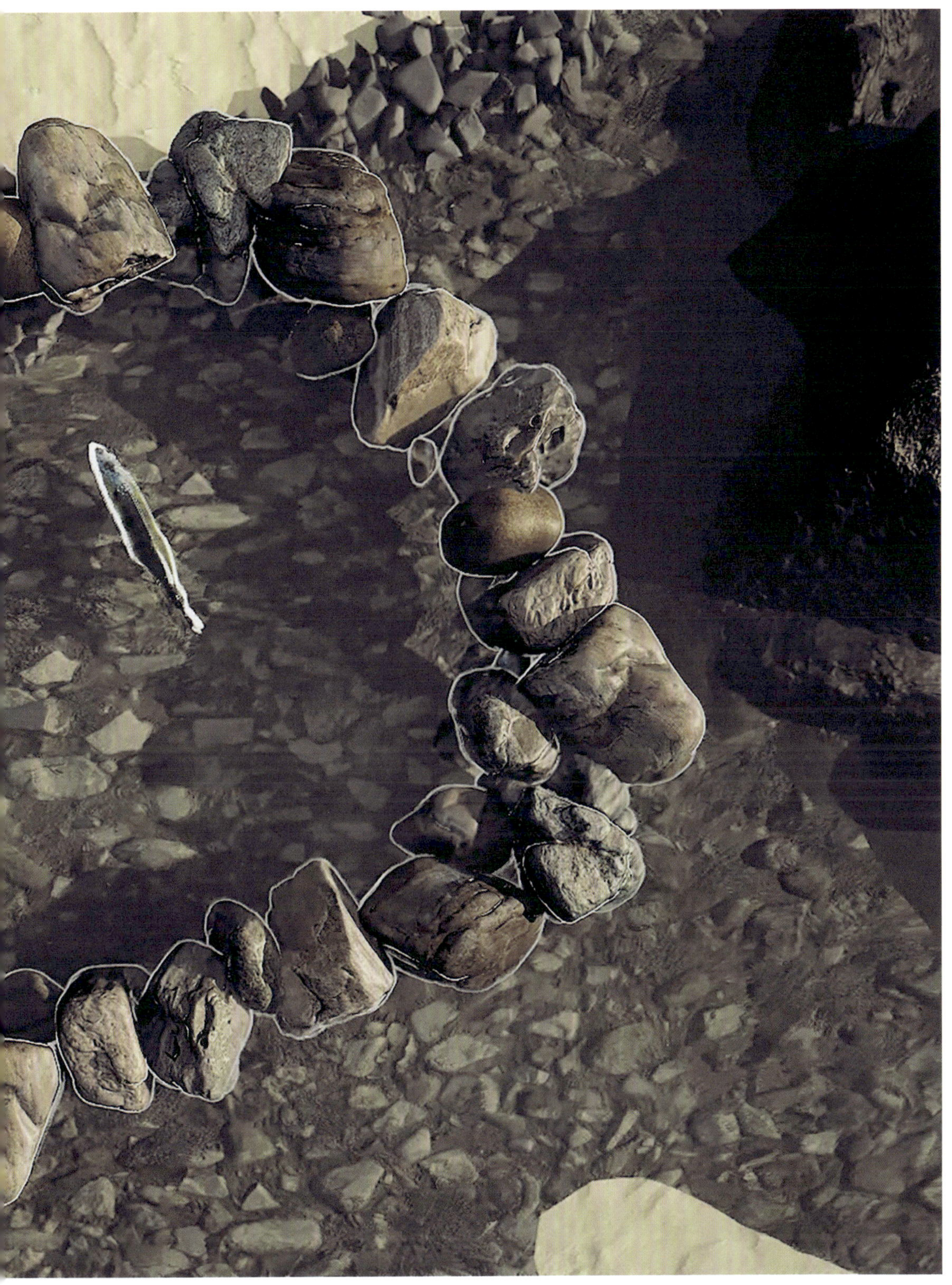

Brad Darkson

One person picks up a rock with the help of another and places it down in a circular formation, a cool sensation up to the knee, waiting for the tide...

How did we get here? Rewind to the beginning.

Kurlannaintyerlo – curl up that sea, on the crest of a wave. Creation is in the now.

Kakirra, the Moon, physically pulls the ocean upwards as she passes overhead in a planetary collaboration. Saltwater moves against rock, slowly eroding minerals to form our oceans. Yarta, the Earth, inhales. Oceans rise. An ancient fault line slowly folds a layer of rock over an eternity. Glacial mudstone deposited from a time defined by cold, formed through eons of immense pressure and elevated temperature. Exhale as oceans recede.

Fungi digest rocks to provide soil for plants. Bacteria provide oxygen to create atmosphere. Each new multispecies community assembled in the process of collaborative world-making and survival.

Tending. Listening to Country. Kaurna bring kardla, fire, to yarta, collaborating with grasslands, trees and other living things that overlap in these *ecologies*. Kakirra passes overhead.

Kauwi, water, rises to the heat. The silence of young shoots underfoot. Freshwater drains from deep rooted grasslands into a gently flowing stream, yawning to meet saltwater, and new collaborations take place. Ceremony. Sing to the ocean. A spring nearby guides the path of the stones into a circular formation. World-making continues.

Enter the *economy* > *oeconomia* > *oikonomia* > *oikos* (house) + *nemein* (manage). Ideas of progress and looking to a *better future* for humanity. One full of promise and ease powered by economic advancement and capital. Humans external to the environment. Industrial progress. Move forward. Forget the present. Kakirra passes overhead.

Humanist and rationalist ideas that centre science and reason over the spiritual and the non-human place emphasis on the individual – consciousness, agency. Our attention drifts further from the collaborative nature of survival in world-making. Survival becomes about the individual. The human species in a growth economy. Humans external to the environment. A new identity of place formed through modernity and progress, and *ownership* of Country. Enormous rock structures take the place of smaller ones for the sake of profit.

Ignore the present. Forget the past. The rocks remain unmoved. Waiting, as kakirra passes overhead.

Today we ask ourselves what lead us to the precipice of ecological catastrophe. Still we push on. Forward. Disconnected from the present. Searching for technological collaborations that might extend our survival in the wreckage of a global economy. A virtual ghost of a time that was present and is now past.

One person picks up a rock with the help of another and places it down in a circular formation, a cool sensation up to the knee, waiting for kakirra.

Are you a morning or a night person? Oddly enough I think I am probably both. I really like the crisp feeling of walking early in the morning and the smell of the night air changing with the rising sun. There is something special about waking up and being up before everybody else is rushing off. But I am always up late working on creative projects, and one of the great things about growing up and living on Kaurna Country is that you're looking west over the ocean where the sun sets.

Is there a sound or song that prompts a where or when for you? There are so many! The first that comes to mind is 'Treaty' by Yothu Yindi, mainly because I am working with this track for an upcoming exhibition, so I've been listening to it a lot lately. 'Treaty' reminds me of my childhood. As a kid I spent a lot of time with my brother sitting in the back of Dad's VL Commodore station agon, listening to cassettes when travelling between Mum and Dad's place.

Is there something you've always collected? Instruments like guitars and I collect a lot of tools.

Where do you feel the most connected / where do you feel the most disconnected? I feel most connected to the Kaurna coastline and being close to the ocean, and I feel disconnected in most city environments; for me there's an undercurrent in cities that usually gives me a feeling of disconnect or imbalance. Also on aeroplanes because there's no concept of space or time.

What scares you the most right now / what inspires you? What scares me most would be the state of the climate and the way that a majority of people think about it.

Through the process of making your new commission for *Between Waves*, what has been revealed and/or become more obscured? A number of aspects of culturally significant sites have become more clear to me through talking to Community and Elders during the development of this commission, and my connection to Country and culture has also become more clear.

Matthew Harris

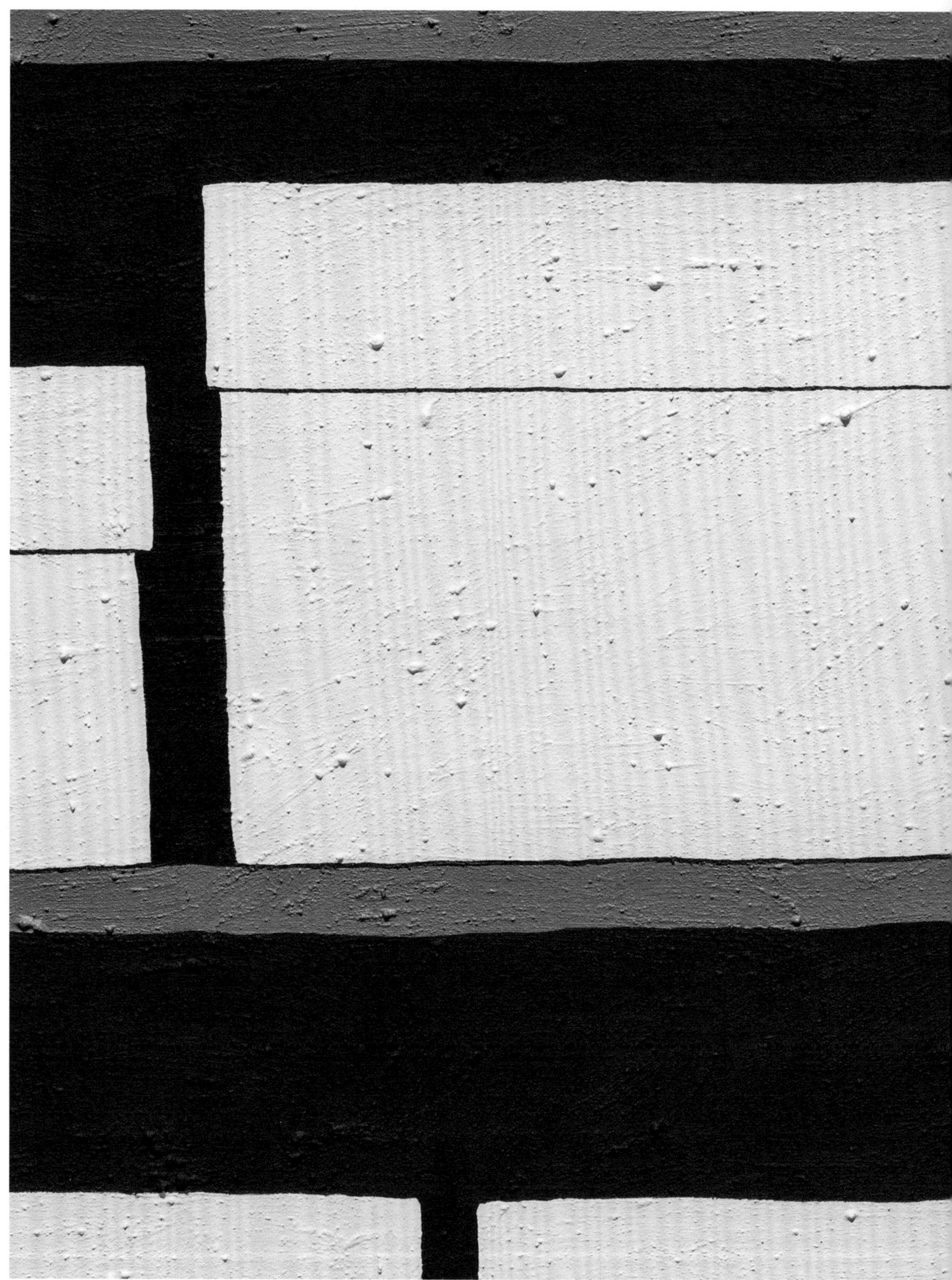

Matthew Harris, *Consigned to oblivion* 2023 (detail)

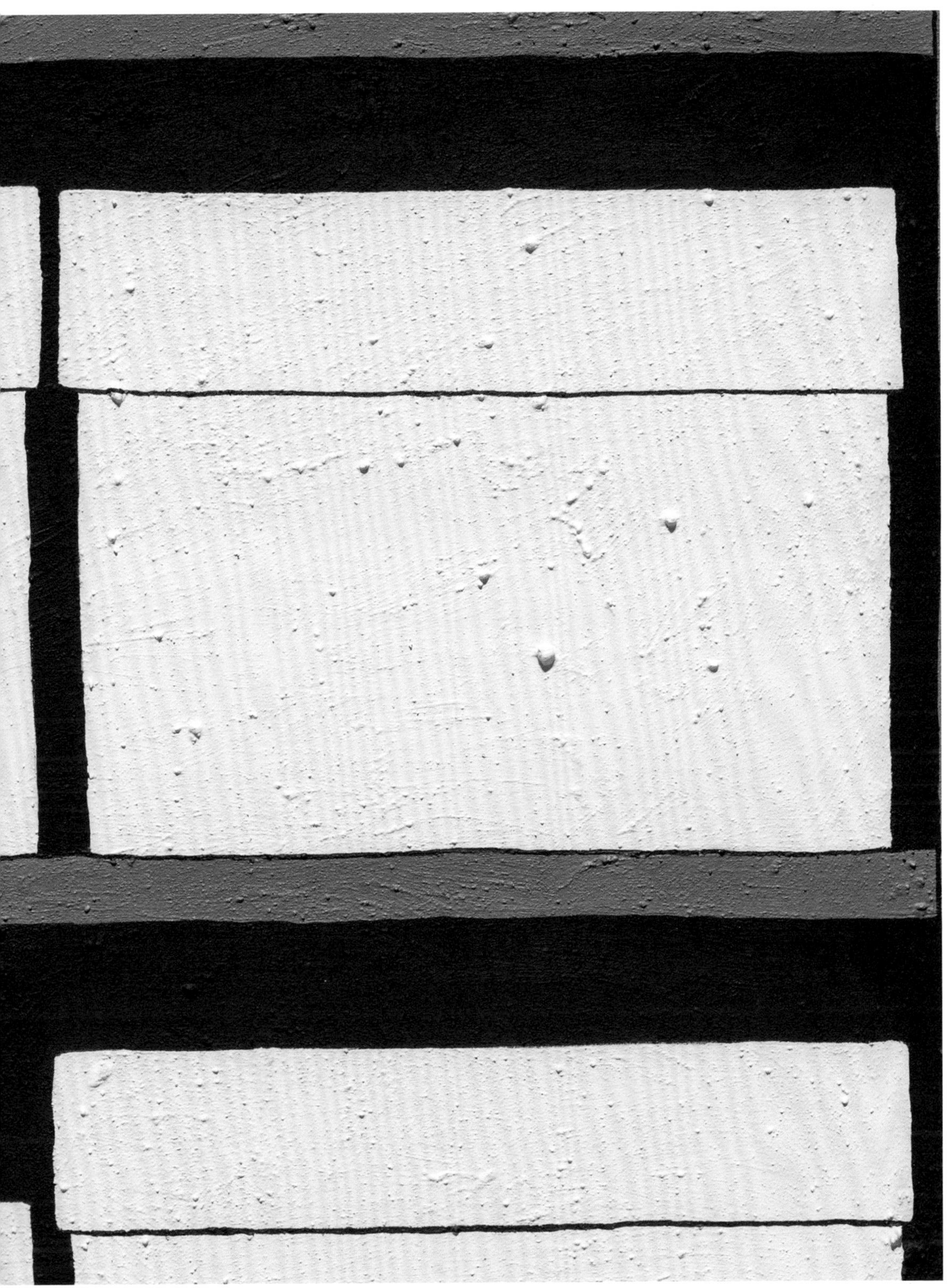

Matthew Harris

Overseas I encountered an Aboriginal skull in a display about human evolution. Tourists shuffled past barely looking at the objects in the cases, most just trying to find the dinosaurs or a toilet. More interesting than the skull itself was the incorrect institutional framing of the skull as a relic of a bygone species and a brief pitstop on the road to modern human, a missing link. The journeys ancestral remains take to end up in a display case on the other side of the world are often long and needless to say, illegal. Mob have continued to campaign for repatriation since the bone trade began, yet tens of thousands of ancestral remains are still concealed in public and private collections without much hope of ever returning home.

Consigned to oblivion 2023 is a monumental suite of paintings spanning the width of the gallery wall. From afar they're the type of monochromatic, repetitive, minimalist paintings you might find at a contemporary art museum such as Dia: Beacon, up close the lumpy surface reveals the texture of their material – crushed charcoal and white ochre, white ochre being most commonly used for sorry business. Far from pure abstraction, the paintings depict a museum storage facility with endless shelves of archival boxes containing bones held in institutional limbo. Blank white facades suspending ancestral remains, sacred objects and cultural heritage behind layers of impenetrable bureaucratic control.

Are you a morning or a night person? Yes.

Is there a sound or song that prompts a where or when for you? The sound of television blaring transports me back to the commission houses I grew up in. The sound of Vanessa Carlton's 'A Thousand Miles' transports me to the movie White Chicks. The sound of puppies transports me to heaven. The sound of Styrofoam transports me to hell.

Is there something you've always collected? Receipts from art expenses, documents from institutional archives, my baby pageant trophies, needlepoint tapestries, Esme Timbery, various rocks. I really need to throw some things away.

Where do you feel the most connected / where do you feel the most disconnected? Connected: anywhere as long as I go walkabout every day. Disconnected: anywhere I'm replying to emails.

What scares you the most right now / what inspires you? A stranger elbowed me in the chest and shoved me into a wall on my way to the studio today, daily life can be pretty scary for a fag in a 1995 Comme Des Garcons coat. There is no hope.

Through the process of making your new commission for *Between Waves*, what has been revealed and/or become more obscured? This work really took it out of me, I think I need to go have a nap.

James Howard

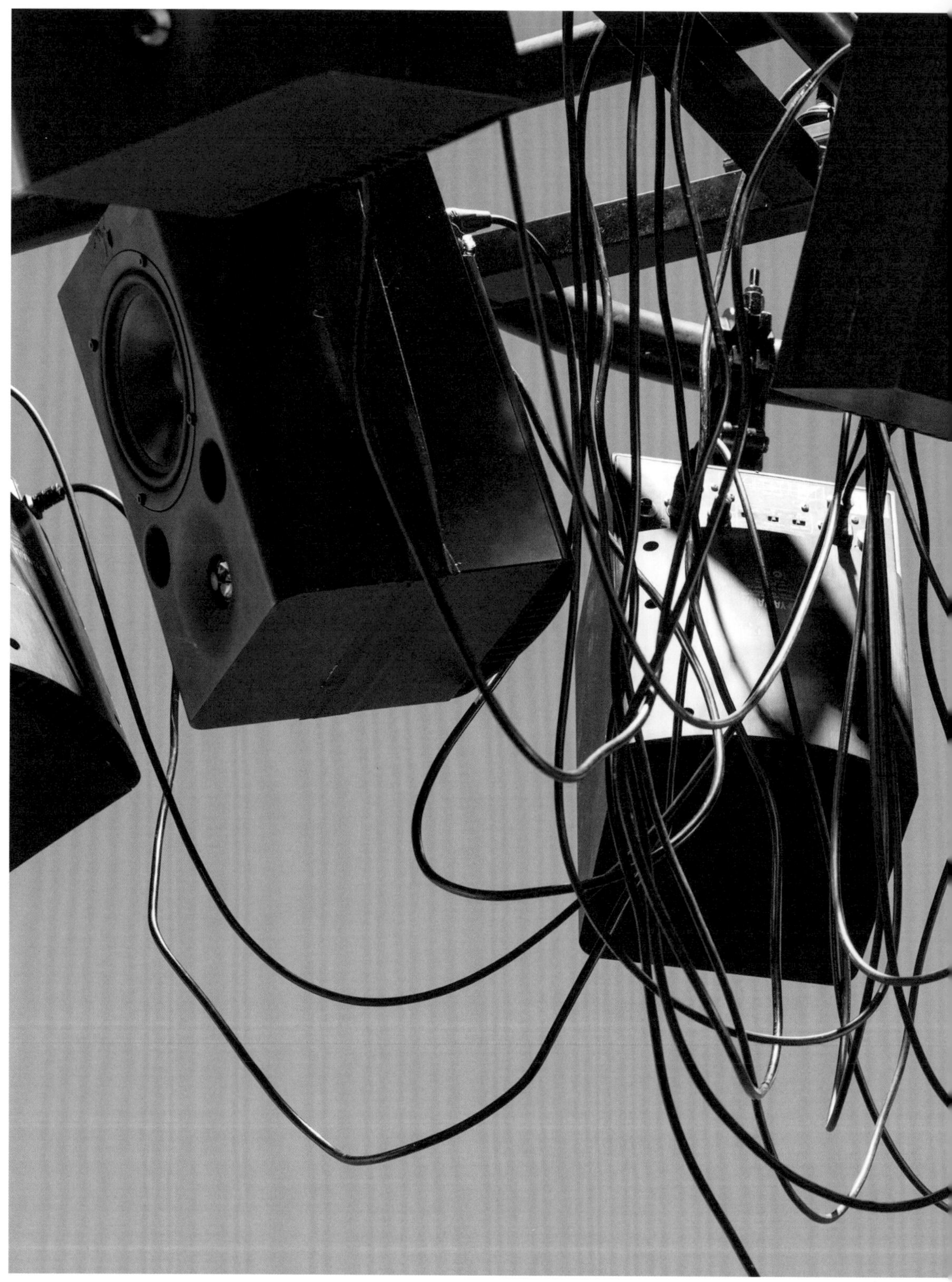

James Howard, *Subterranean frequencies* 2023 (detail)

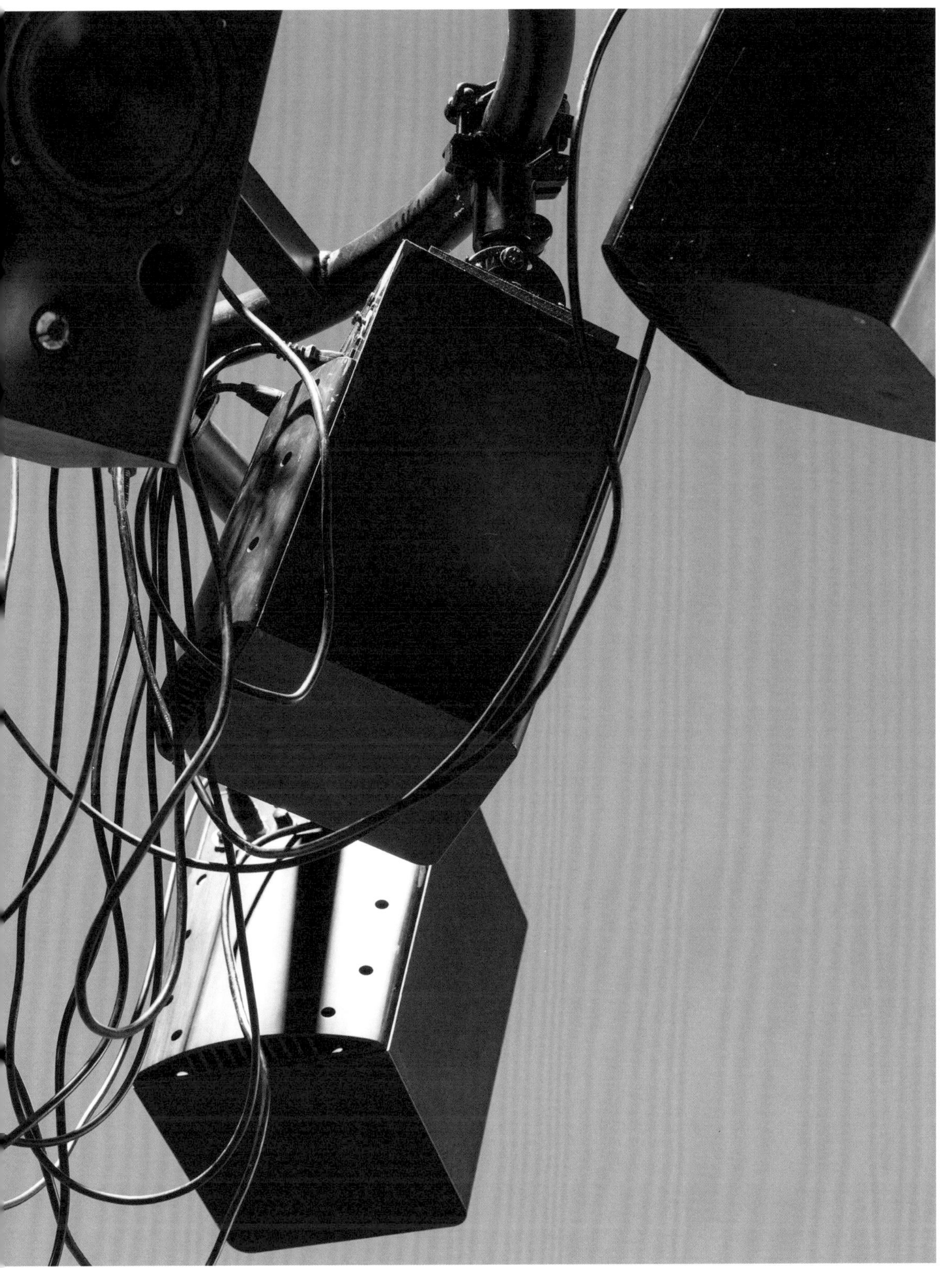

James Howard

This is a transmission beamed to you from beyond the borderline. Stories are waiting to be heard. In this room sound is an aesthetic experience. The work is immaterial yet it takes up space and evokes movement in a way that is immeasurable and illogical.

Subterranean Frequencies 2023 invites you to focus on the fringes. The work exists at the meeting place between waves of the tangible and the intangible. It holds a microphone to the hidden places that are passed by each day.

Sounds were captured and composted from a network of tunnels located below the surface of the gallery to tell stories that are always present but rarely heard. Raw audio was recorded in the Mezzanine, a giant underground cavern located beneath ACCA's building. The condenser microphones responded to the ambience of the underground space, activated by ventilation shaft hums and whistles reflecting off of high cement ceilings; the contact microphones were affixed to metal surfaces and machinery, which vibrate with the sympathetic resonance of cars passing through the nearby Burnley Tunnel; and wideband receivers snatched elements of electromagnetic radiation from the air.

Sound becomes malleable. Recordings are stretched and compressed. A single snapshot in time is reworked into an endless drone. A moment can last forever. The heard and the unheard are brought together in a collage — amplified into the industrial soundscapes within which we are constantly immersed.

Just as these hidden spaces dot our lives, so too do the stories of place dot the Country upon which we all walk. Stories that are still waiting to be heard.

Is anyone receiving them?

Are you a morning or a night person? Morning.

Is there a sound or song that prompts a where or when for you? There is a field recording of birdsong I made out on Jaadwa Country in the northern Gariwerd back in 2019. The next year, when the city was living through the deepest stretch of the lockdown, I used to put it on and marvel at the way these recordings could transport me 300km away to that little patch of land.

Is there something you've always collected? Music. I still can't bring myself to stream music. I like to discover my music by rifling through record store racks, researching performers, discussing my latest finds with friends and family, and building a little library of albums that speak directly to me.

Where do you feel the most connected / where do you feel the most disconnected? My favourite time of the week is when I'm going nowhere fast on a weekend morning. I'll sit back with a fresh cup of coffee, and a slab of wax on the turntable. I would say that's when I feel most connected to myself.

What scares you the most right now / what inspires you? Like most Millennials, I have been grappling with an ongoing existential crisis since I was a little fella, so there's very little that scares me now that I haven't previously considered. That said, working on this piece for *Between Waves*, at least I now know where to hide and restart society from when the bomb drops (hint: it's about three-metres beneath the exhibition).

Through the process of making your new commission for *Between Waves*, what has been revealed and/or become more obscured?I don't think I can answer this question until the exhibition is open to an audience. A lot of the work I do stems from a process of putting my thoughts and ideas on a public stage and getting a reaction. In that sense, I cannot know how the piece resolves until it is no longer just mine to enjoy.

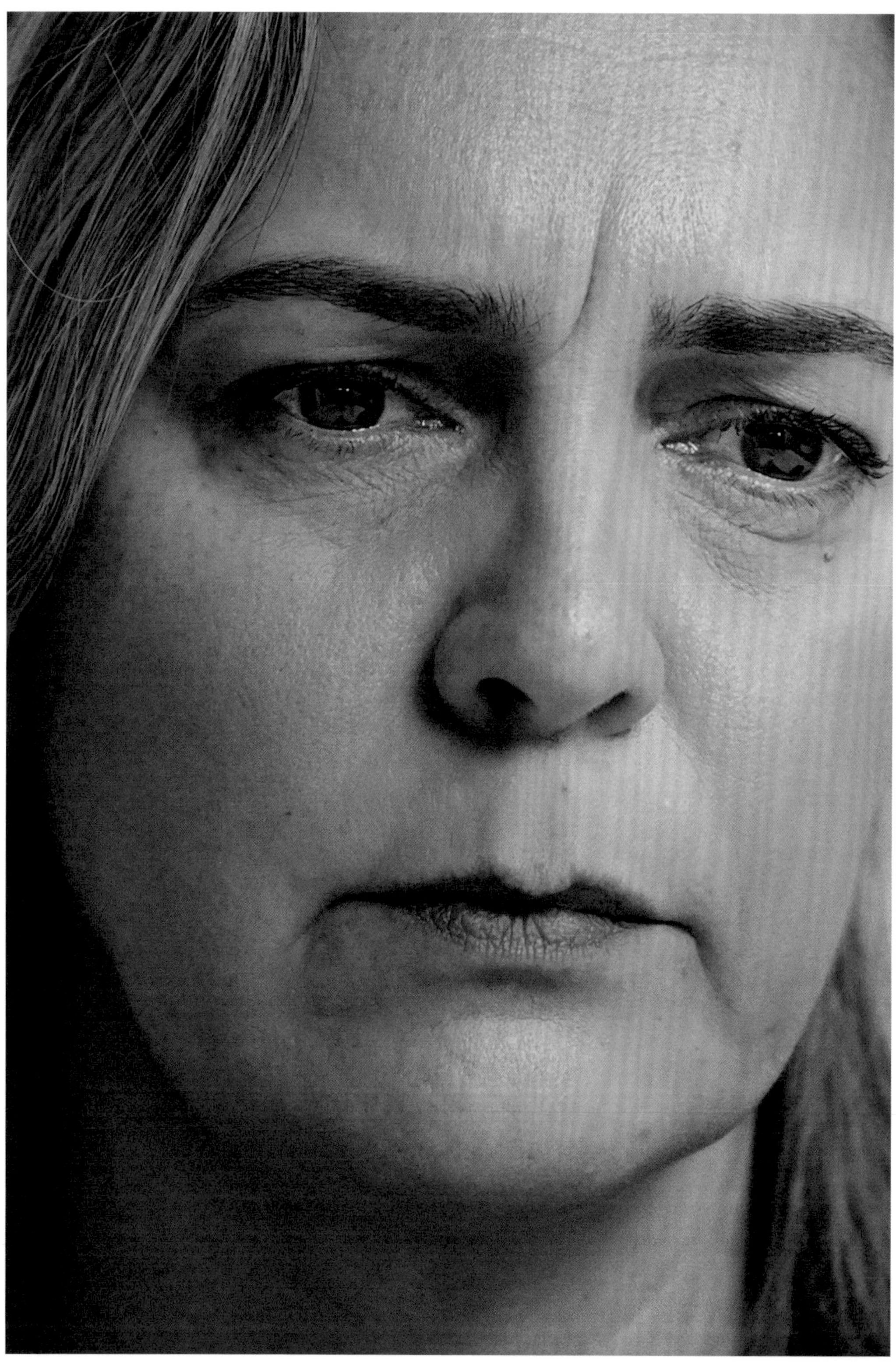

Left and right: Hayley Millar Baker, *Entr'acte* 2023 (stills)

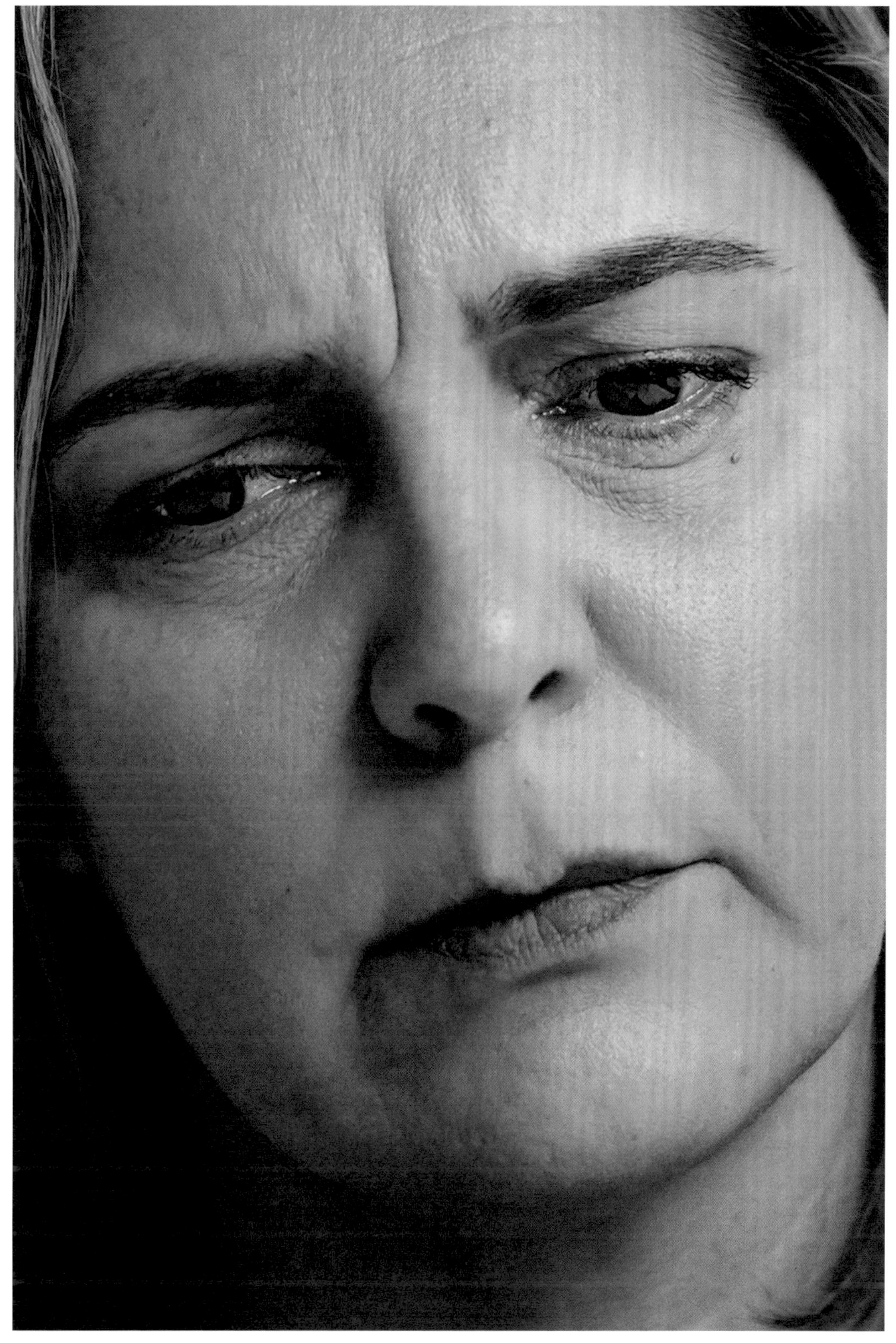

Hayley Millar Baker

Entr'acte channels the internal feelings of restrained rage and its transformation into grief, rippling through the body and permeating all levels of the self. Taking its title from the French word 'Entr'acte' – referring to an interlude performed between two acts of a play – the work centres a female protagonist cast as a vessel symbolising 'woman' who is holding the inequitable weight women are forced to carry and contend with daily, across the multitude of experiences, identities, and roles they play. *Entr'acte* simultaneously embraces notions of intimacy and intensity to convey the monumental focus, determination, and power of women, capturing the moment after an action and before a reaction, or external rupture. Neither documentary, nor fiction, *Entr'acte* raises a pertinent social commentary about the expectations forced on women – mourning the loss of free expression in a world of social and cultural inequity.

> 'The pain of women turns them into kittens and rabbits and sunsets and sordid red satin goddesses, pales them and bloodies them and starves them, delivers them to death camps and sends locks of their hair to the stars. Men put them on trains and under them. Violence turns them celestial. Age turns them old. We can't look away. We can't stop imagining new ways for them to hurt.' – Leslie Jamison, 2014[1]

1 Leslie Jamison, 'The Grand Unified Theory of Female Pain', *The Virginia Quarterly Review*, Spring 2014, Vol. 90, part 2, 2014, viewed 8 June 2023, https://www.vqronline.org/essays-articles/2014/04/grand-unified-theory-female-pain.

Are you a morning or a night person? I am a night person, I do my best thinking at night, but I have children who are up at 5am. So, I'm forced to be a morning person too.

Is there a sound or song that prompts a where or when for you? The Cure, 'Close to Me'. For me that is the one of the songs of my childhood, dancing and singing in the lounge room with my cousins and Aunties.

Is there something you've always collected? When I was younger, I used to collect mini Buddhas I don't know why / I throw out things that no longer serve the time I am in.

Where do you feel the most connected / where do you feel the most disconnected? Most connected in my dreams / least connected in the physical world.

What scares you the most right now / what inspires you? I've recently learnt I'm scared of earthquakes since the two earthquakes in Victoria in the past year / Art history inspires me, it's where I look to when I need to get a fresh perspective.

Through the process of making your new commission for *Between Waves*, what has been revealed and/or become more obscured? The thing that has become clearest to me through the process of making this commission, is that no matter what I thought I wanted the work to be, the work had its own idea of what it needed to be, which was a bit scary. I had all these grand ideas and then none of that worked and it just needed to be what it wanted to be. I have never worked in that way, never put a strait cut into anything. The work needed to be what the work needed to be, and I had to lean into that.

Jazz Money

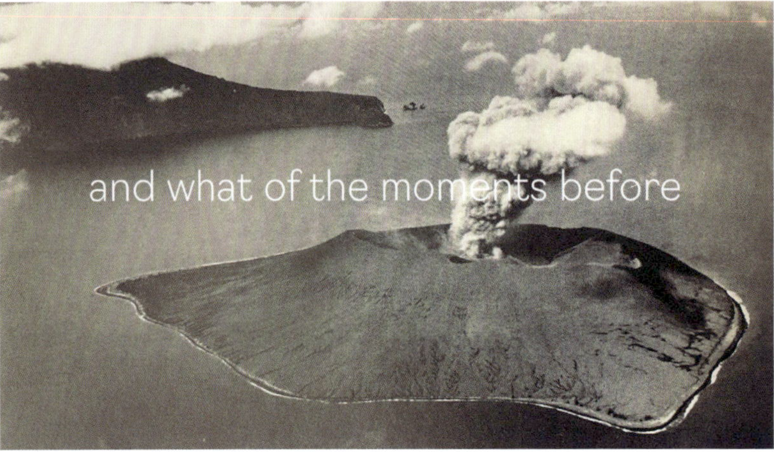

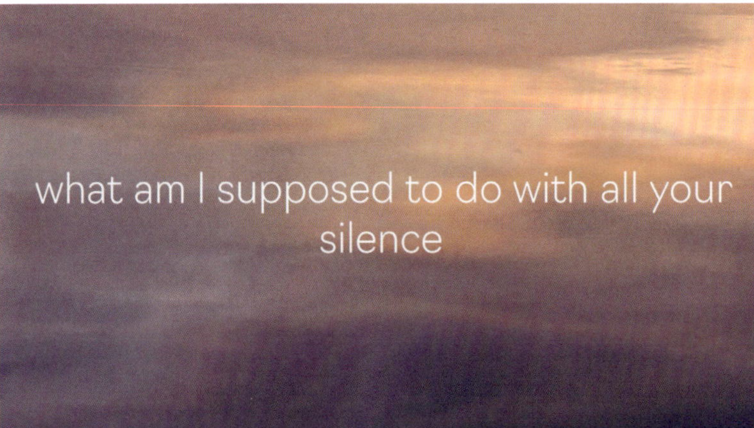

between the shac

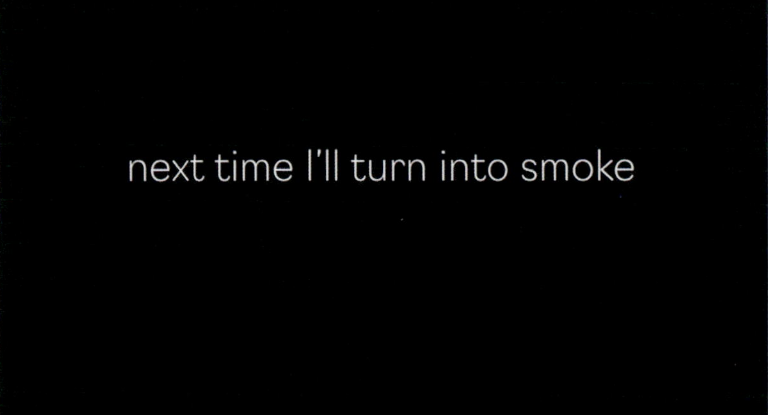

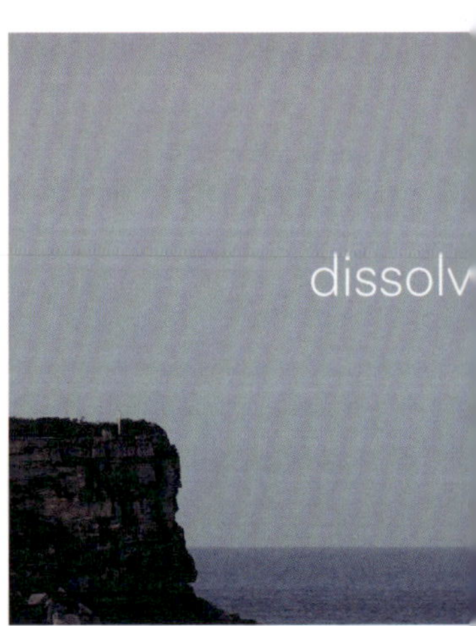

Jazz Money, *infinite iterative piece* 2023 (stills)

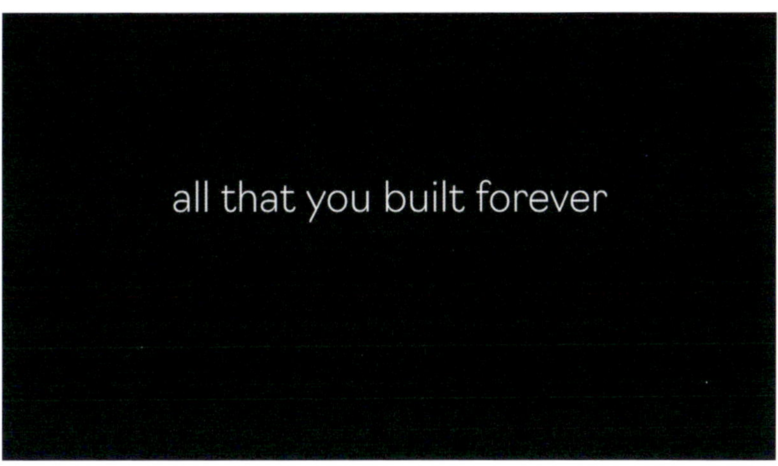
all that you built forever

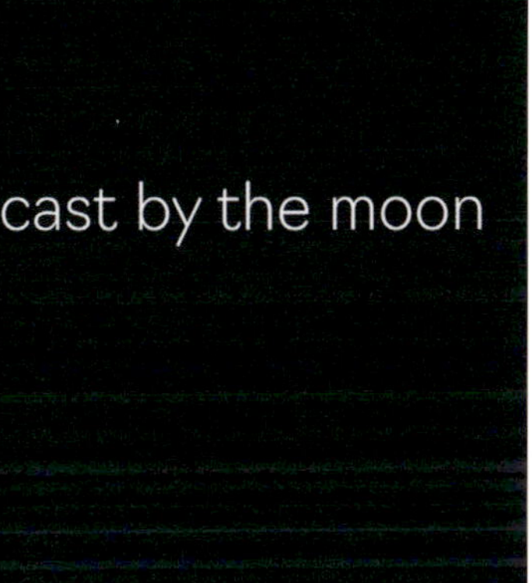
cast by the moon

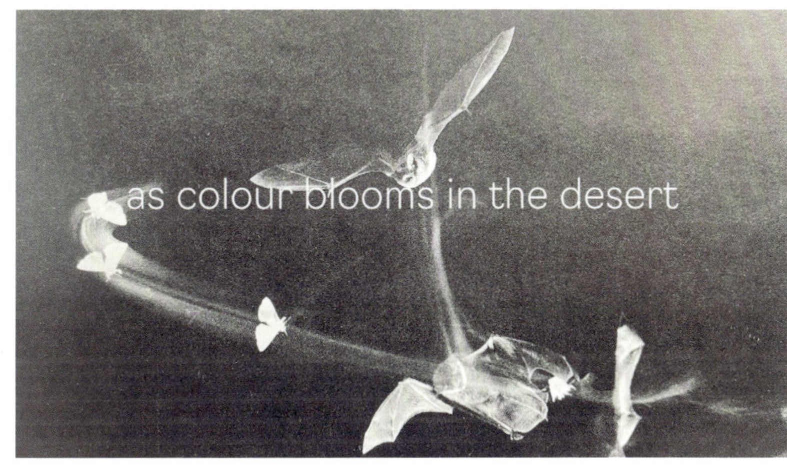
as colour blooms in the desert

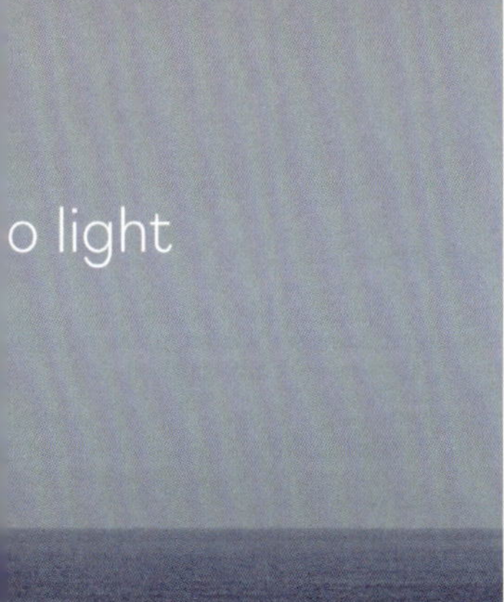
o light

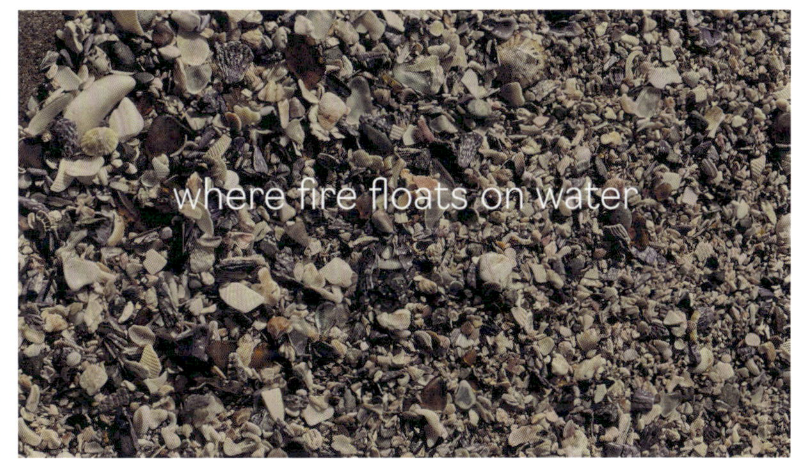
where fire floats on water

Jazz Money

infinite iterative piece welcomes you to find what you didn't know you were seeking. A poem created just now, just for you, appearing through chance and hope and randomising software. *infinite iterative piece* is compiled of all the lost lines that didn't become poems, the photos and footage that feel more like poetry, the ideas that shouldn't go together, and the narratives that they tell.

Presented across three screens the words and images chop and change in a randomised configuration creating new experiences for each viewer. The screens create something of a digital 'exquisite corpse' where neither creator nor audience know what will be revealed in any single moment. The work can continue to grow and expand as more lines are added with time, a vessel for infinite questions and answers.

The work brings together two enquiries by the artist – poetry and film – and in particular the synergies between these mediums. Both poetry and film editing in particular take a preexisting language or set of images and arrange them in complimentary, contrasting or contradictory ways to communicate something to an audience. In that pairing, you create a third space where new knowledges are revealed.

By presenting the work in this randomised way, *infinite iterative piece* reflects both the overload of content and imagery that exists in our world, and the very human desire to make meaning of all that input. The poetics of life often reveal themselves to us in surprising ways, and *infinite iterative piece* seeks to be a gift for audiences looking for pause and beauty within the chaos.

Are you a morning or a night person? I am an aspirational morning person but it doesn't always come naturally.

Is there a sound or song that prompts a where or when for you? Oh so many! Different bird songs remind me of being a kid growing up in the bush. Pop songs transport me to who I was when I first heard them. Different languages remind me of travels or friends. I am a very nostalgic person so I love revisiting past experiences through different sensory invitations.

Is there something you've always collected? I have collecting (hoarding) tendencies – my work for *Between Waves* is sort of about that exact impulse. Ever since I was small I've especially loved collecting bits of paper, vintage postcards, old books, notepads and any sort of 2D scraps. Now I often justify holding onto these things for potential artworks, but as yet I haven't made any work from them!

Where do you feel the most at connected / where do you feel the most disconnected? Bodies of fresh water are my favourite place to be. I don't assume that I am necessarily always welcome and so I go gently and listen deeply, but when I feel a welcoming connection those special places are always my favourite.

What scares you the most right now / what inspires you? I have huge climate anxiety and am deeply afraid of impending climate collapse. But I am inspired by the love, care and responsibility First Nations mob from around the world have for our Countries and believe that will be the only thing that can truly save us from disaster.

Through the process of making your new commission for *Between Waves*, what has been revealed and/or become more obscured? Making *infinite iterative piece* has given me a place to put an endlessly long list of lines, ideas and images. Leaving things to chance has made me feel more relaxed in how to engage with these things: to relinquish them to the world and to allow process to lead.

Cassie Sullivan

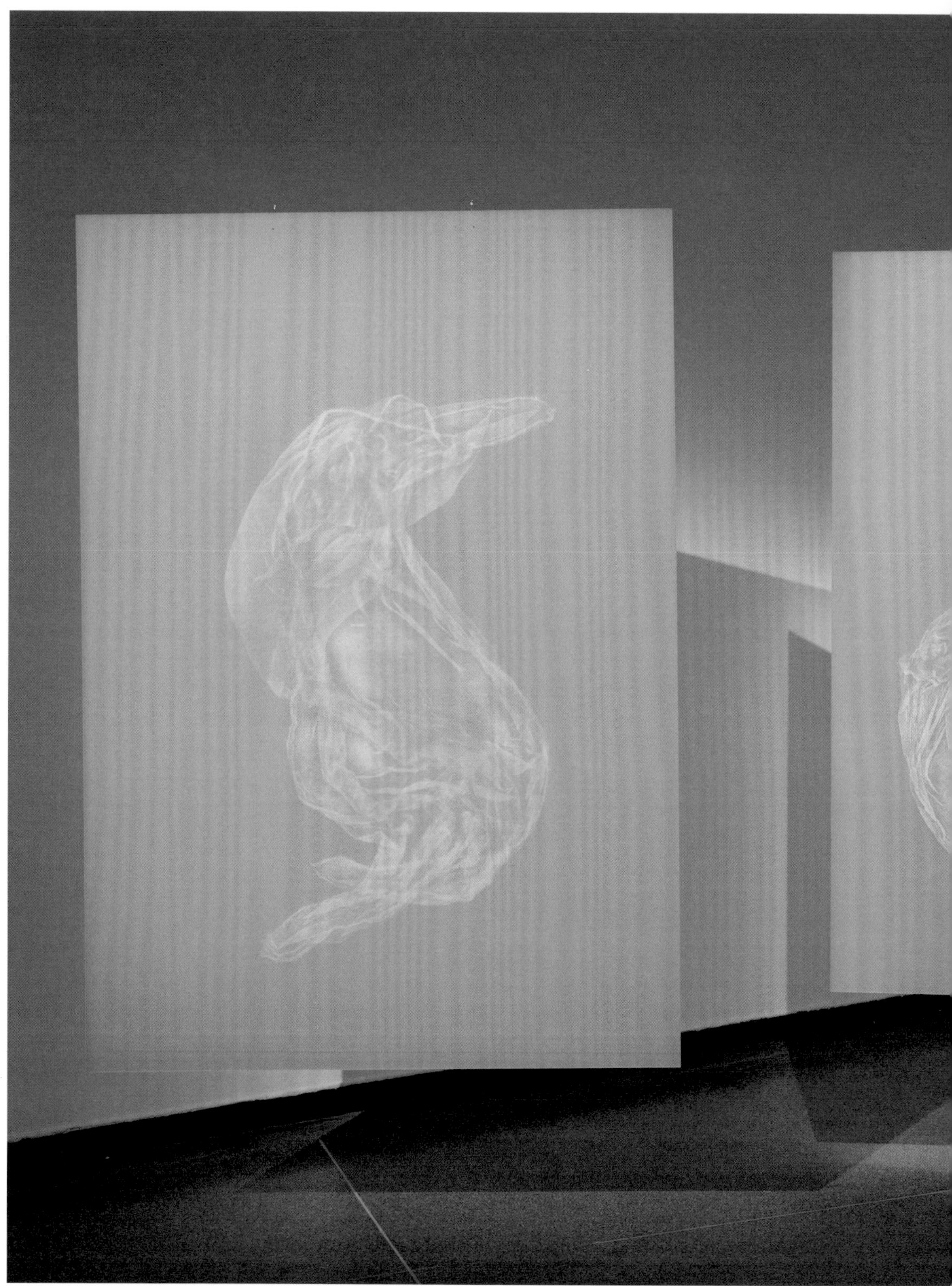

Cassie Sullivan, *wayi (to hear)* 2023, installation view

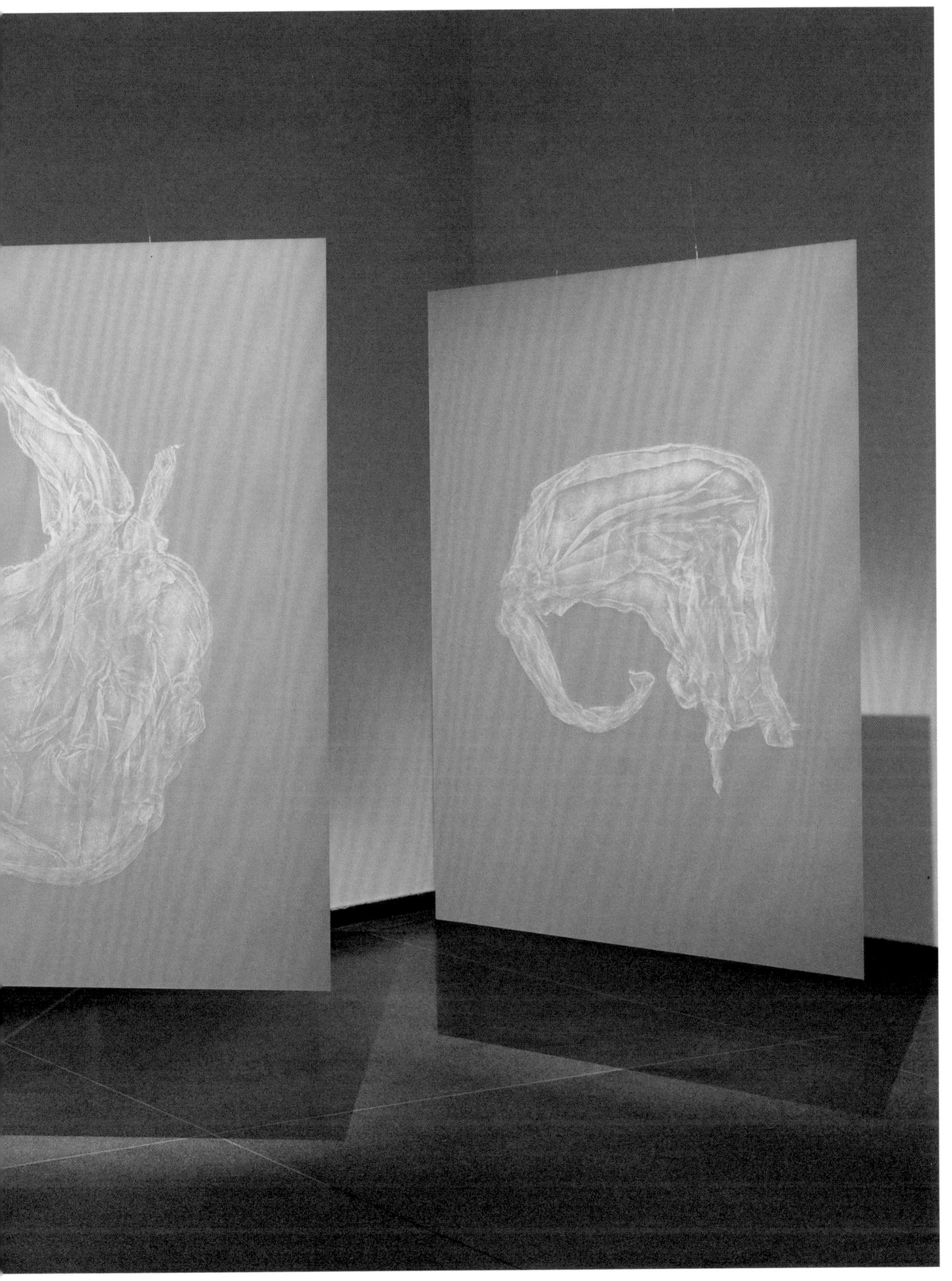

Cassie Sullivan

i have drowned here
in these waters
of brine
and salt
and preservation

The ancestors hang here. Float, suspended in the neverwhere and the everywhen.

A succession of experiences, of traumas, of attempted erasures. Those forced to sacrifice ceremony for survival.

Country holds a space for them here, will always know them. And I hold them here, in my sinew and my skin.

They cried that they needed healing in the only language I knew how to hear.

I took a piece of tarlatan, a cloth of care, of wound mending, and I threw it into the sea. The only place I've ever felt home.

I have pulled and pushed the tarlatan through our waterways, watched it breathe in the tidal inlets. Letting in the tannins from the mountains, letting out the brine. Swallowing the language of salt and blood-stained water.

I meet them here, in the intertidal drifts of the melukerdee and nuenonne. And I listen. Collecting knowledge of place, relearning a somatic language, growing a vocabulary of grief.

As I work the ink and salt-soaked tarlatan into each monotype, I embed myself here too, in these pieces that are the height of me, in this material, that has been torn to my proportions. My muscles ache at the work being done. The imprinted narrative shifts alongside me.

Positive, negative.
Present, missing.
Floating, bound.

I walk amongst the hauntings of transgenerational communication.

My body remembers them.

Are you a morning or a night person? I am a night person. There is something very particular about the arrival of the dusk light that makes my body stop and take notice of the landscape around me.

Is there a sound or song that prompts a where or when for you? The calls of the mangana, the yellow tailed black cockatoo brings me straight home, both physically and metaphorically. I can feel my head lift and my shoulders drop as soon as I hear them.

Is there something you've always collected? I'd have to say photos. I first turned to photography in an attempt to document feelings of place and people, I'm still on that journey. It helps me take the time to connect with people and culture and there is something inherently precious in the memories a printed photograph represents.

Where do you feel the most connected / where do you feel the most disconnected? I feel most connected when I can see the ocean, it's a curiously grounding space for me, full of depth and opposing natures. I feel most disconnected when I'm away from family, I can operate separately from them, but it doesn't feel quite right.

What scares you the most right now / what inspires you? I think the dangerous, untrue and unfair rhetoric around queer and trans people is what scares me the most currently, along with the ability for a majority public with no skin in the game to make decisions that deeply affect people's lives. The thing that brings me the most hope is the unique stories of open minded and big-hearted people in my life. I have so many inspiring people I get to interact with daily. I feel so lucky to have conversations about the complex layers that can be held within this existence.

Through the process of making your new commission for *Between Waves*, what has been revealed and/or become more obscured? It's become clearer to me that my practice is trying to give voice to those who are part of the lost generations. My ancestors and the stories of those in my community that haven't always been given a platform to tell their histories of being hidden, adopted out, renamed, erased from documentation, shamed, dismissed etc. It's becoming more and more important for me to acknowledge them and hopefully heal our ancestral lines by doing so. This quickly becomes complex in the current climate of politicisation of indigenous bodies and the identities they hold.

this mob

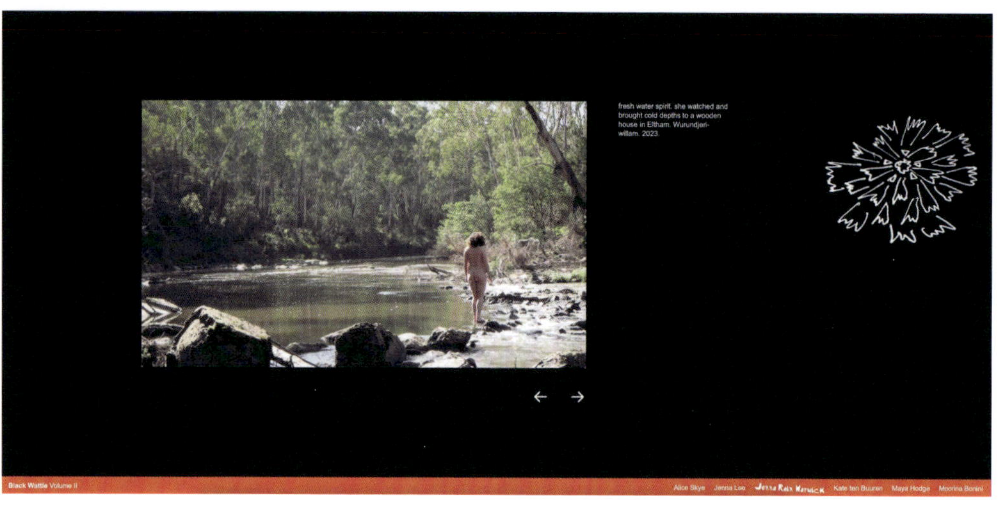

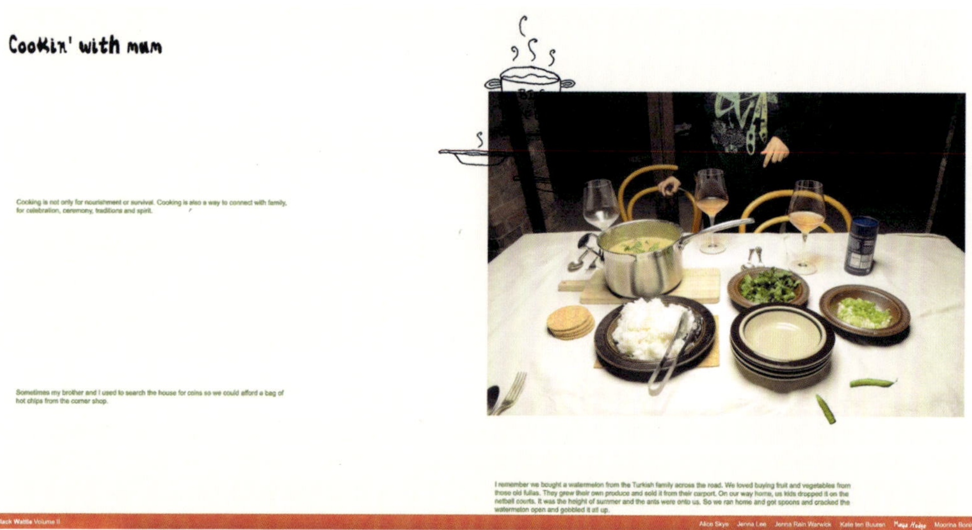

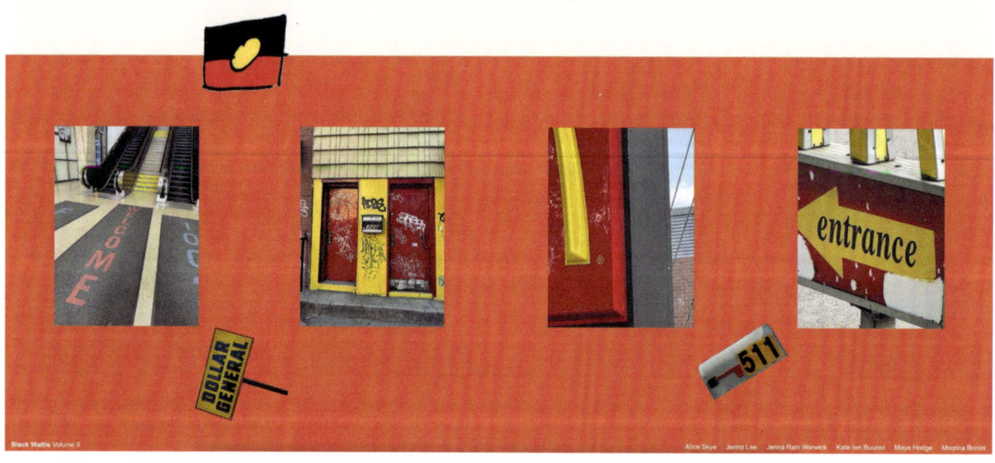

this mob, *Black Wattle Volume II* 2023 (digital commission)

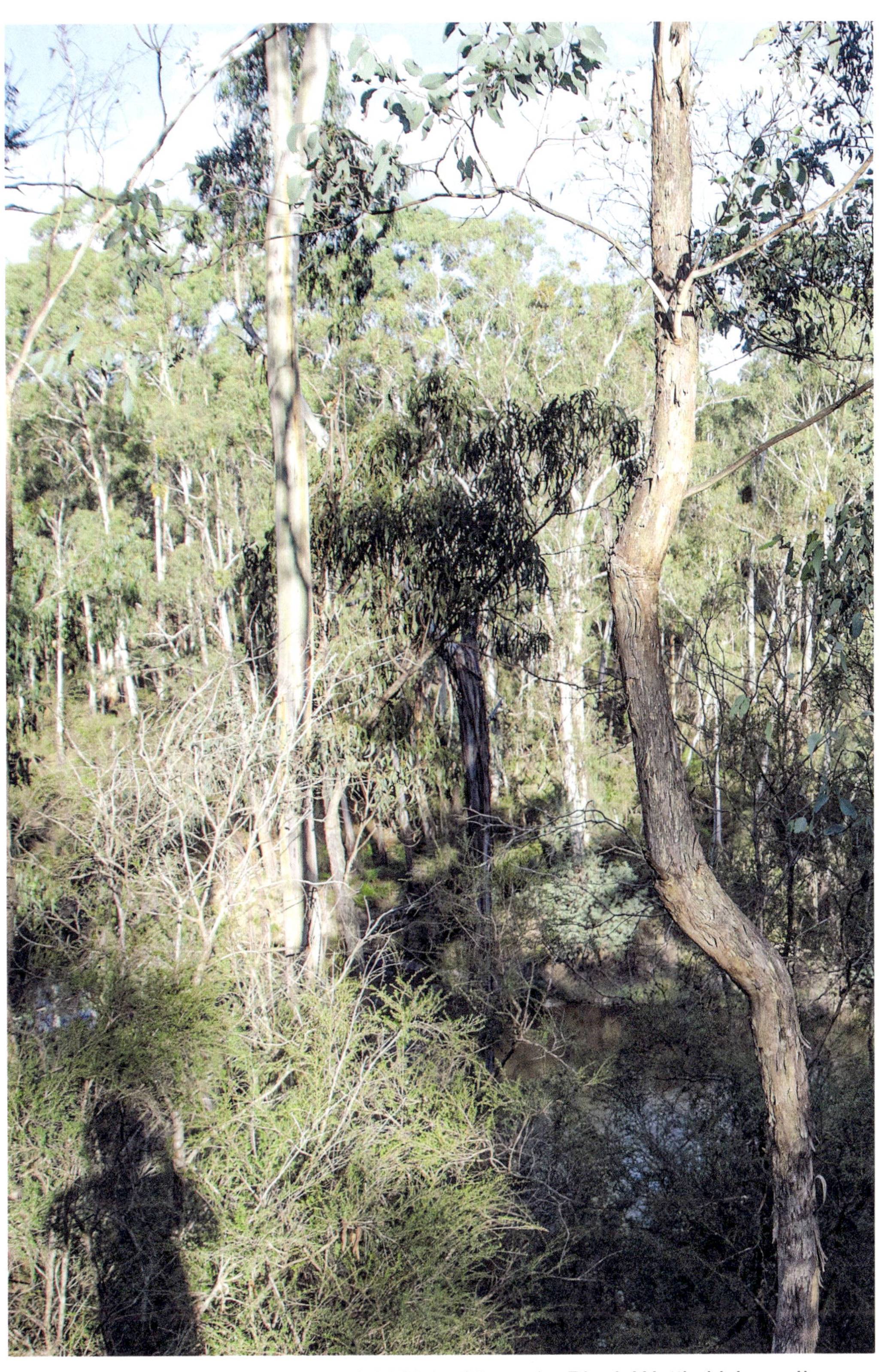

Moorina Bonini, *Molwa (shadow)* 2023 in this mob, *Black Wattle Volume II* 2023 (digital commission)

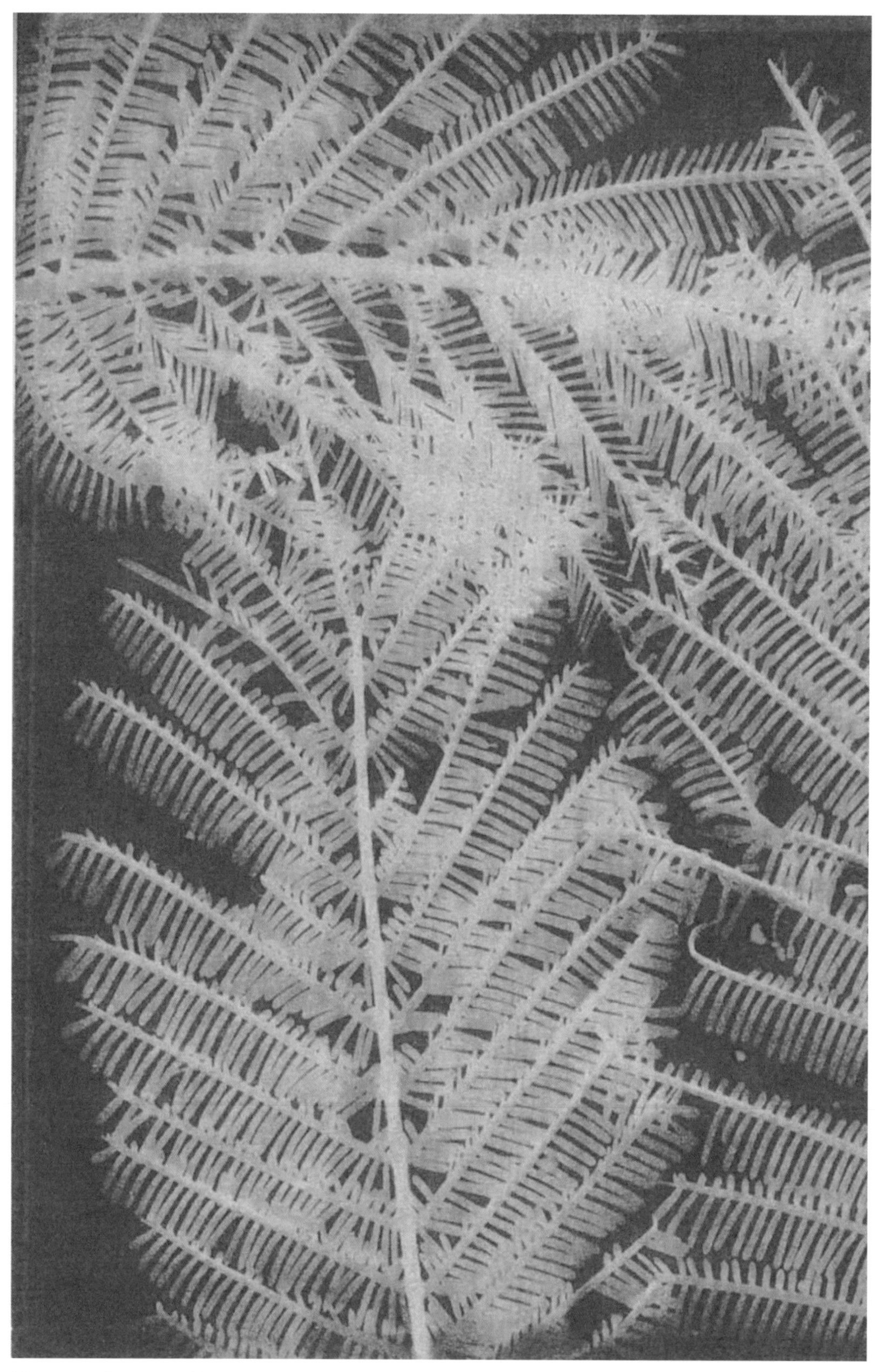

Kate ten Buuren *Untitled* 2023 in this mob, *Black Wattle Volume II* 2023 (digital commission)

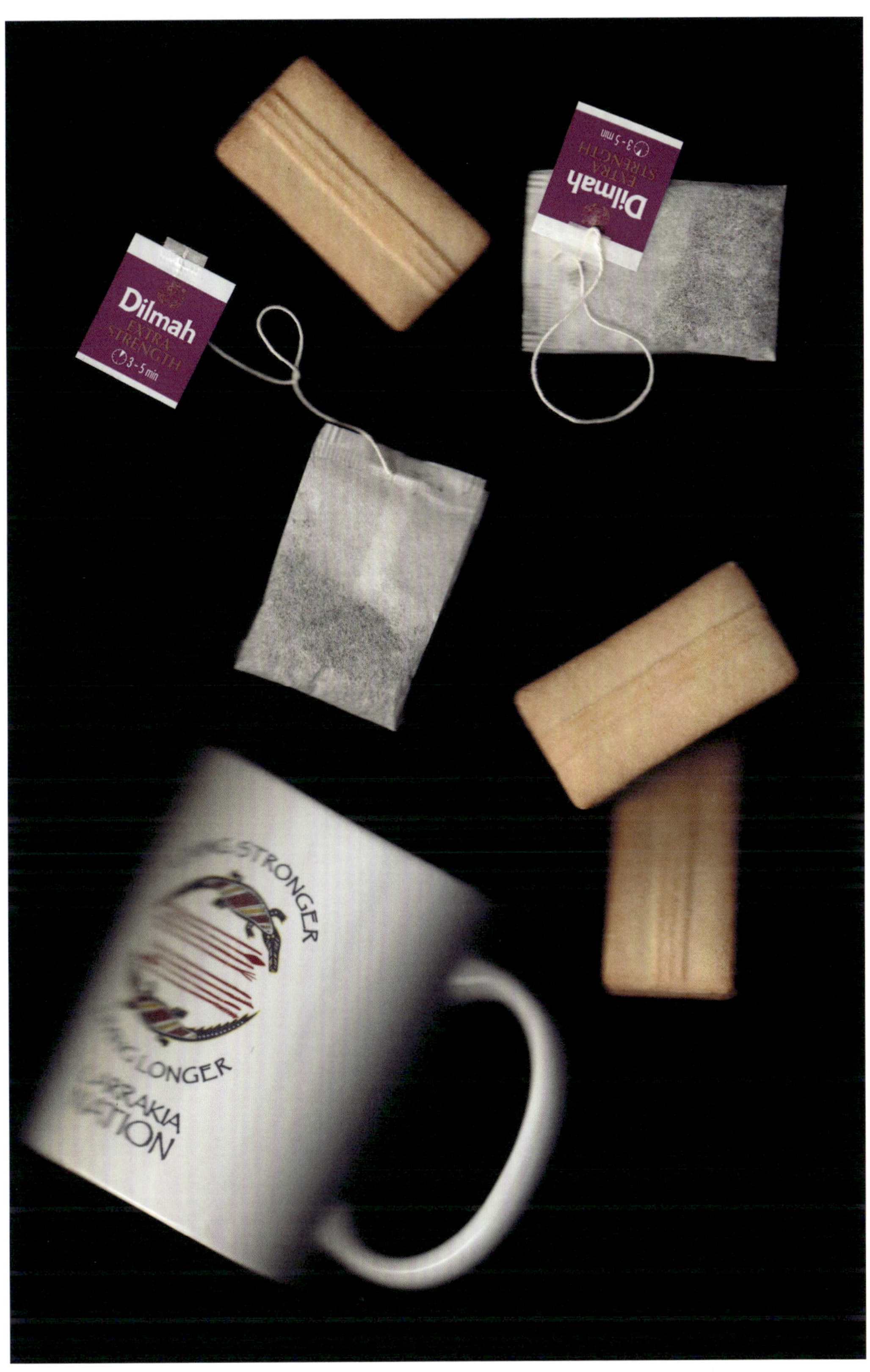

Jenna Lee, *Cure For Distance 1* 2023 in this mob, *Black Wattle Volume II* 2023 (digital commission)

this mob

MB: *Black Wattle Volume II* is a collection of thoughts and reflections of what it means to be connected within a blak collective while also being connected to Country and community. Our threads of connectedness are made evident through making and yarning amongst ourselves, and across our individual works. Each of us holds a thread that connects us back to our own ancestral lands, to our own histories, our own knowledges and families. The digital space becomes an interface between ourselves; a space where we can speak to and from. The molwa (shadow) has always been an interest to me. An extension of self onto Country - a presentation of self. This showcases the relationship between our bawu (body), mulana (spirit) and woka (country) - each is entwined and connected. They do not work in separation from each other instead, bawu, mulana, and woka work together to form ourselves.

JRW: Spying on them in the kitchen, listening to them talk. I thought I was the one sneaking and listening until Maya found me by the eel trap. We couldn't decide if we would go back the easy way or the hard way until we realised we didn't know the difference. It's funny as I think about being watched and also onlooking, I wasn't a part of original volume of *Black Wattle* but I was around... hearing about it, talking about it. I feel like the way we work allows me to swim through.... *Black Wattle Volume II* is just about us, and in a way it allows us to talk and be together. I made a horror style shaky short film, Maya was the protagonist. It's vaguely about a water spirit that watches from the outside, until a certain time at night when the veil between the outside and inside is porous. The more patience, the less we plan and just be. I feel most inspired, it is strange also thinking that others outside of this mob will read, watch and listen to *Black Wattle Volume II* as it feels private, I think that having it online puts me at ease. Not that any of the content is made for our eyes only, just that it seems very personal.

KTB: I wasn't with you all for the fire yarns, and I was trying to look for home in the places I was travelling through while overseas, that were so different (and sometimes familiar) to home. I collected photos of all the red, black and yellow combinations in the changing landscapes. While I was home, I made a work on Country while camping with my family - exposing materials from Country to the sun and washing them in cold Taungurung waters. The works were made while thinking about the ways we connect over space and time, whether we are on Country or very far away. *Black Wattle* is always a time capsule or document of where we are, at the time we're making - sometimes unresolved, and sometimes just an experiment. I invited Alice to make a cryptic crossword just for mob. She made me one for a Kris Kringle gift on Christmas and it was the most special present, it's nice to have something just for us, that you know is handmade, and thought about to make you smile and feel special. Lots of homely vibes.

JL: For me, *Black Wattle Volume II* was a chance to make just for me/us, which I think is why my work is so much more personal than usual. There is so much support within the collective to simply make the works we wanted, it's amazing to have a platform where they can be shared together. My work is really reflective and about moments of connection with people around food and drink. While I was too sick to be away together for our residency, viewing everyone's works really helped me think about what matters to me about being a part of a collective/ family. My series Cures for distance shows three digital scans of food/drink that comfort me when I am missing people.

MH: Creating this second iteration of *Black Wattle* has been full of restful moments. Sitting together with Moorina and Jenna Rain up on Wurundjeri Country in front of the fire until the early hours felt like I could breathe deeply again. Being in the city for such a prolonged period of time impacts my ability to create and think up new ideas. Slowing down and cooking everyone a chicken curry from a recipe my mum emailed me made my heart full. This time away allowed me to reflect on my childhood and how coming together to share a meal is more than the nourishment from the food, its nourishment from the people you share it with too.

Are you a morning or a night person? KTB: Morning! I'm always hassling these mob with messages first thing in the morning.

Is there a sound or song that prompts a where or when for you? JRW: crows always remind me of the highway and hot days with not much to do.

Is there something you've always collected? JL: I collect (hoard) so many things — feathers, books, trinkets — always with the justification that one day I might need them for art.

Where do you feel the most connected / Where do you feel the most disconnected? MB: The studio. this mob: Yeah!

What scares you the most right now / what inspires you? MH: All of the above, the morning texts from Kate.

Through making your new commission for *Between Waves*, what has been made clear and/or become more obscured? this mob: We realised we want to do more residencies — we loved the process of being together — and that is the work.

Mandy Quadrio

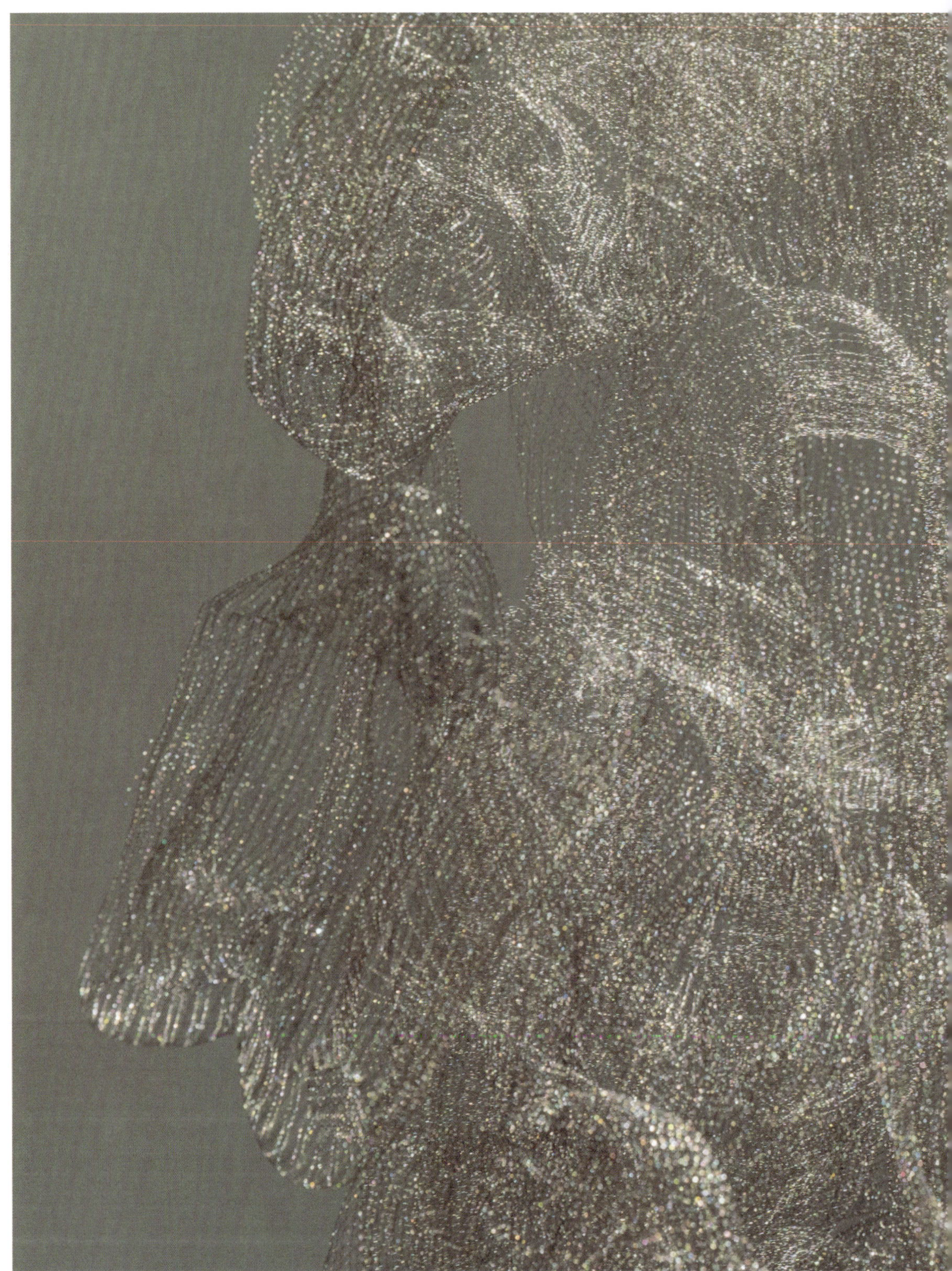

Mandy Quadrio, *Not gone!* 2023 (detail)

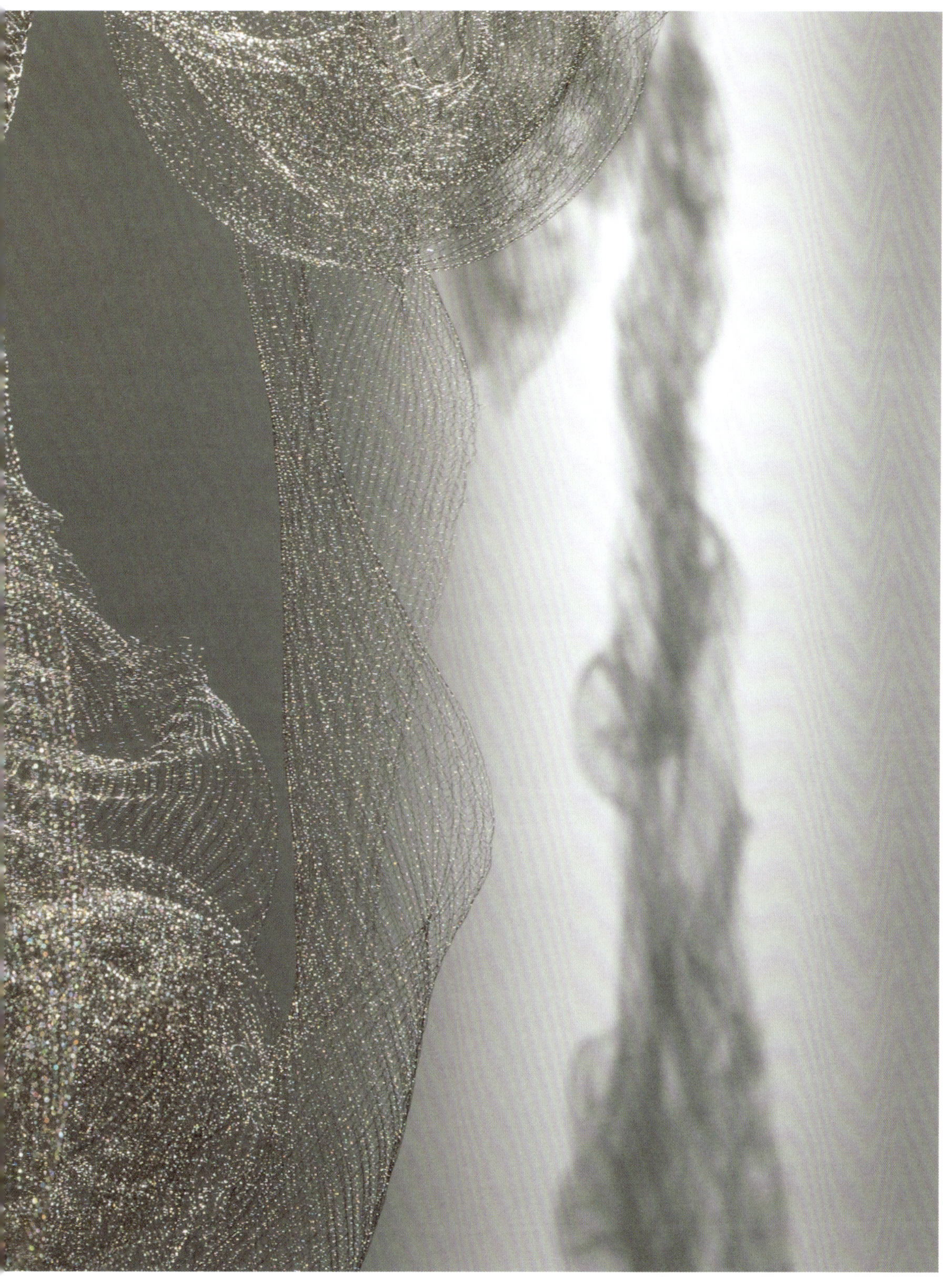

Mandy Quadrio

As a Trawlwoolway and Laremairremener, Tasmanian Aboriginal woman, I am moving beyond the limitations of controlling aspects of Australian histories that remain shrouded in false and obscured narratives.

Using steel and wiry fibres, I seek to weave experiences, memories and stories that move and change through time. I manipulate netted, steel wire-mesh forms, anchoring my stories to demonstrate and assert my Indigeneity, adaptability and strength, and my long-time relationship to land, Country and culture.

Light and motion work to activate and illuminate the sculpture's sparkling, wire-mesh material. Suspended, sinuous, and tactile shapes are cast with light to enliven and to allow the works to perform — their movements create illusions of density despite their significant lightness of being.

As the shadows from the work move in and out of focus, they provide transitory moments that sometimes evoke bodily forms and other presences. I value my connections to entities – both past and present. I do not step away from my own history and experiences.

Within mutable, shadow-filled spaces, the sculptural forms appear smooth and sleek, belying the sharpness of their steely, abrasive fibres that have the potential to incise and open shared wounds. I use the steel fibres to reference abrasive acts and unhealed traumas that are outcomes of colonisation. I choose to journey through and beyond wounding's to carefully enfold the complexities of harsh histories and actions that have been historically and contemporaneously enacted on Australian Indigenous people.

The ongoing mistelling of Australian history manifests as a cultural amnesia. Such disremembering seeks to make Indigenous Australians invisible. I am Not Gone!

I invite viewers to position themselves within the shadowy fibres of this work and to cast light on their own knowledge of Australian Indigenous histories.

Are you a morning or a night person? I am definitely a night owl. Is there a sound that prompts a where or when for you? The sound of thunder sees me running for cover — I'm terrified of it.

Is there a sound or song that prompts a where or when for you? The sound of thunder sees me running for cover — I'm terrified of it.

Is there something you've always collected? Three things that I have always collected are antique or vintage floor rugs, particularly rugs with a history and that have been well trampled; and because I grew up in Papua New Guinea I have always had a love for bilum bags. As well as being incredibly strong and functional objects, the bags are true works of art. I also love tea cups — all shapes and sizes because I drink copious amounts of tea... I am learning to declutter to make my life more simple by throwing away objects and things that take up space, especially at home. This means I can store more materials to use in my art practice.

Where do you feel the most connected? / where do you feel the most disconnected? I really feel connected when I am on Country in Tebrakunna, up in the Far North East of Lutriwita (Tasmania). Walking where I know my ancestors have travelled for millenia helps me to feel grounded and anchored to place. I feel disconnected when I am flying in a plane. Flying makes me feel uneasy. I like to have my feet on terra firma.

What scares you the most right now / what inspires you? The plight of the planet really scares me, particularly the ongoing destruction of the natural environment. I live in Meanjin/Brisbane and despair as I watch trees coming down at a rapid rate. Sadly, humans are so disconnected from the natural world. We don't realise that we are all in this together. Despite the fact that Australia is a very racist country, I feel hopeful knowing that younger people now are rejecting the lies of history that we were told as children. Nationally there is a much greater understanding of the notion of Country and the many Aboriginal and Torres Strait Islander nations that have and continue to occupy this land we now call Australia. I am inspired by the fact that through acknowledgements and Welcomes to Country, Indigenous people are now claiming place and space. I am hopeful that the Voice will succeed and bring about more socially just outcomes for Indigenous Australians.

Through the process of making your new commission for Between Waves, what has been revealed and/or has anything become more obscured? When I am making art, every day is a learning process. I am always encountering something new, challenging, or unknown. My work for Between Waves has taught me a lot about working with wire and helped me to understand kinetics and movement in art. Overall it showed me that with perseverance most things are possible. Because in my work there is a large focus on my disappeared mother, while I have come to understand more things about her through my research, at the same time she continues to become more elusive.

List Of Works

Maree Clarke
now you see me: seeing the invisible #1 2023
297 photographic microscopy prints on acetate
30.0 x 30.0 cm each
Created on Wurundjeri and Boonwurrung Country
Courtesy the artist and Vivien Anderson Gallery, Melbourne

now you see me: seeing the invisible #2 2023
video projection
duration 5:53 mins
Created on Wurundjeri and Boonwurrung Country
Courtesy the artist and Vivien Anderson Gallery, Melbourne

now you see me: seeing the invisible #2 is generously supported by Federation Square and Melbourne Arts Precinct Corporation

Dean Cross
On who goes to The Gallows
1997-2023
aluminium, timber, synthetic polymer paint, fired ceramic, fabric and paper
174.0 cm x 316.0 cm x 131.9.0 cm
Created on Walbunja, Wurundjeri and Boonwurrung Country
Courtesy the artist and STATION, Melbourne

Brad Darkson
waiting for kakirra 2023
motion activated animation and HD video with sound
dimensions and duration variable
Community consultants: ngangki burka, Senior Kaurna woman, Aunty Lynette Crocker, Aunty Merle Simpson, Uncle Jeffrey Newchurch.
Research assistants: Des Gubbin, Sue Specks, Yankallila locals and council staff members
Animation artists from ACOLAB, Tarntanya:
Lead animator: Thom Dickson
Modelling: Nathan Hartman
Animation consultant: Arthur Ah Chee
Technical artists: Tom Meakin and Darcy Holmes
Created on Kaurna Yarta
Courtesy the artist

Matthew Harris
Consigned to oblivion 2023
ochre, charcoal, and acrylic binder on linen
198.0 x 167.0 cm each
Created on Wurundjeri Country
Courtesy the artist and FUTURES, Melbourne

James Howard
Subterranean frequencies 2023
4.1 channel sound sculpture
duration: from the time that it is turned on until the time that it is turned off
Created on Wurundjeri and Boonwurrung Country
Courtesy the artist

Hayley Millar Baker
Entr'acte 2023
single channel video
11:20 mins, looped
Director: Hayley Millar Baker
Videographer: Melle Branson
Actor: Clothilde Bullen
Editors: Dylan Timtschenko, Fancy Films
Colour: Peter Hatzipavlis, Final Grade
Created on Whadjak Noongar, Wurundjeri and Boonwurrung Country
Courtesy the artist and Vivien Anderson Gallery, Melbourne

Entr'acte is generously supported by Craig Semple

Jazz Money
infinite iterative piece 2023
three-channel video projection, 16:9
duration variable, audio 9:25 mins looped
Film: Jazz Money
Text: Jazz Money
Audio: e fishpool
Created on Gadigal and Budawang Country, with images and footage captured in Australia, USA, Lebanon, Palestine, India and Italy
Courtesy the artist

Mandy Quadrio
Not gone! 2023
wire mesh, rotating mechanism
dimensions variable
Created on Jagera and Turrbul Country
Courtesy the artist

Cassie Sullivan
wayi (to hear) 2023
seven tarlatan monotype prints on frosted acrylic
170.0 x 122.0 cm each
Created on melukerdee and nuenonne Country
Courtesy the artist

this mob
Moorina Bonini, Maya Hodge, Jenna Lee, Jenna Rain Warwick, Kate ten Buuren
Black Wattle Volume II 2023
digital commission
Website designer: Rio Ramintas
Website developer: Charlotte McLachlan
Cryptic crossword: Alice Skye Anderson
Custom typography: RMIT Master of Communication Design Students; Adelia Jovani, Enshuo Zhang, Guanyu Zhao, Peixin Gao, Ruixue Sun, Satya Darshini Penmetsa and Yanxin Zhang, guided by Courtney Bree and Fayen d'Evie
Created on Wurundjeri and Boonwurrung Country
Courtesy the artists

Black Wattle Volume 2 is generously supported by The Ian Potter Foundation and through the Agency AiR Residency Program hosted at the Garambi Baan Residency Centre operated by InPlace.

This new digital commission has stemmed from this mob's recent publication *Black Wattle* 2021, which received support through Arts House's annual Refuge program.

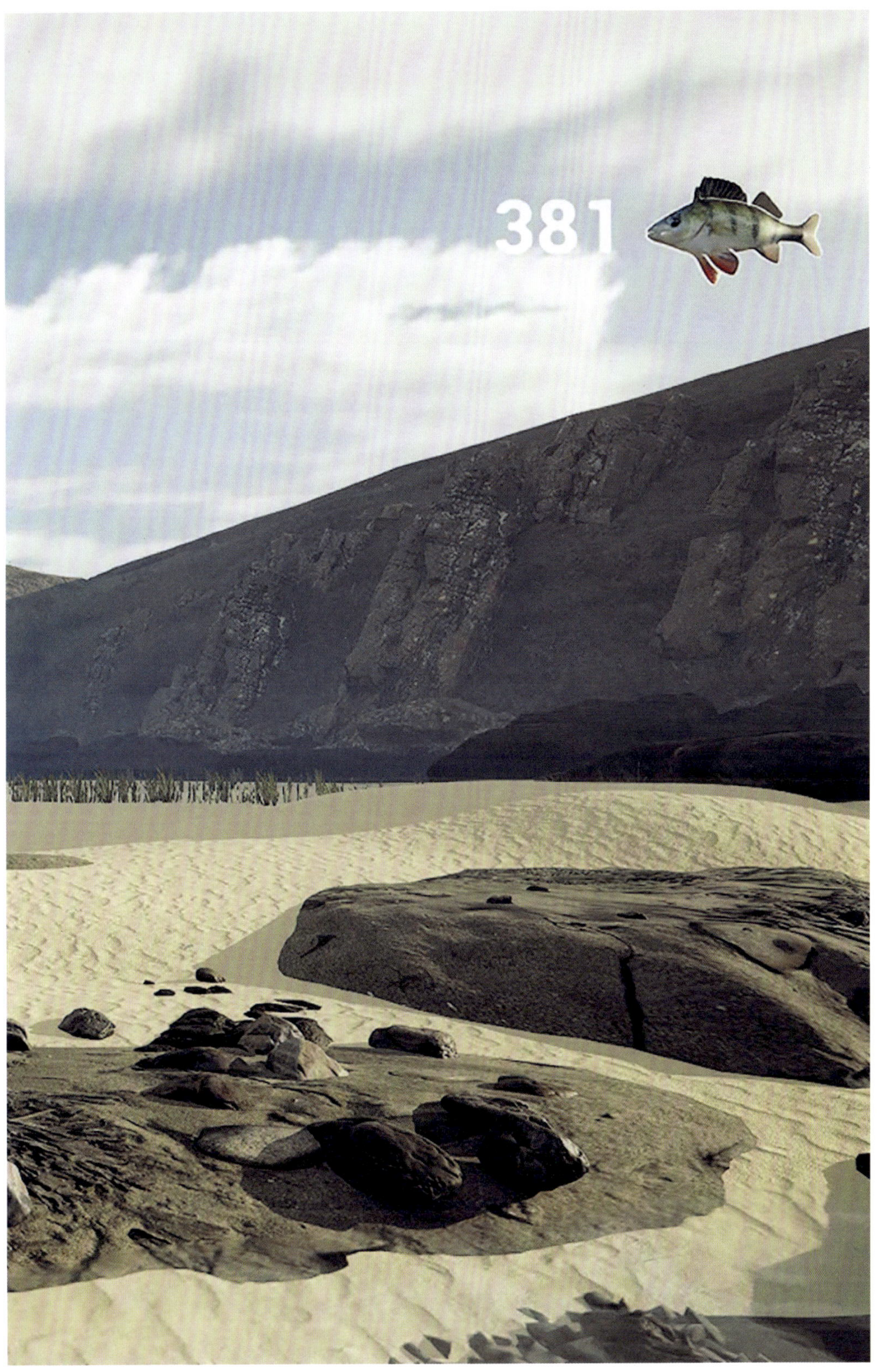

Brad Darkson, *waiting for kakirra* 2023 (detail)

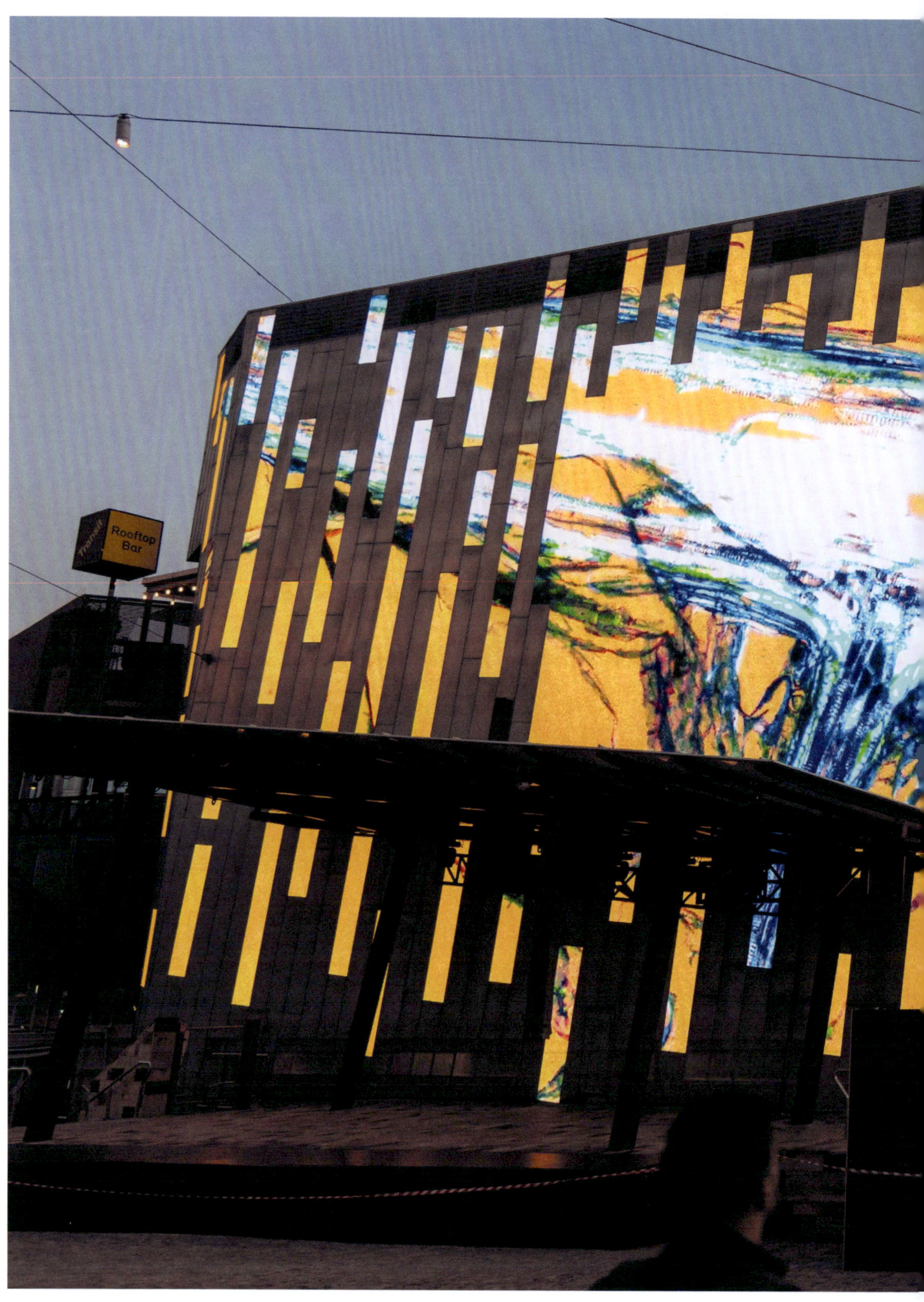

Maree Clarke, *now you see me: seeing the invisible #2* 2023. Courtesy the artist and Vivien Anderson Gallery. Photo: James Henry.

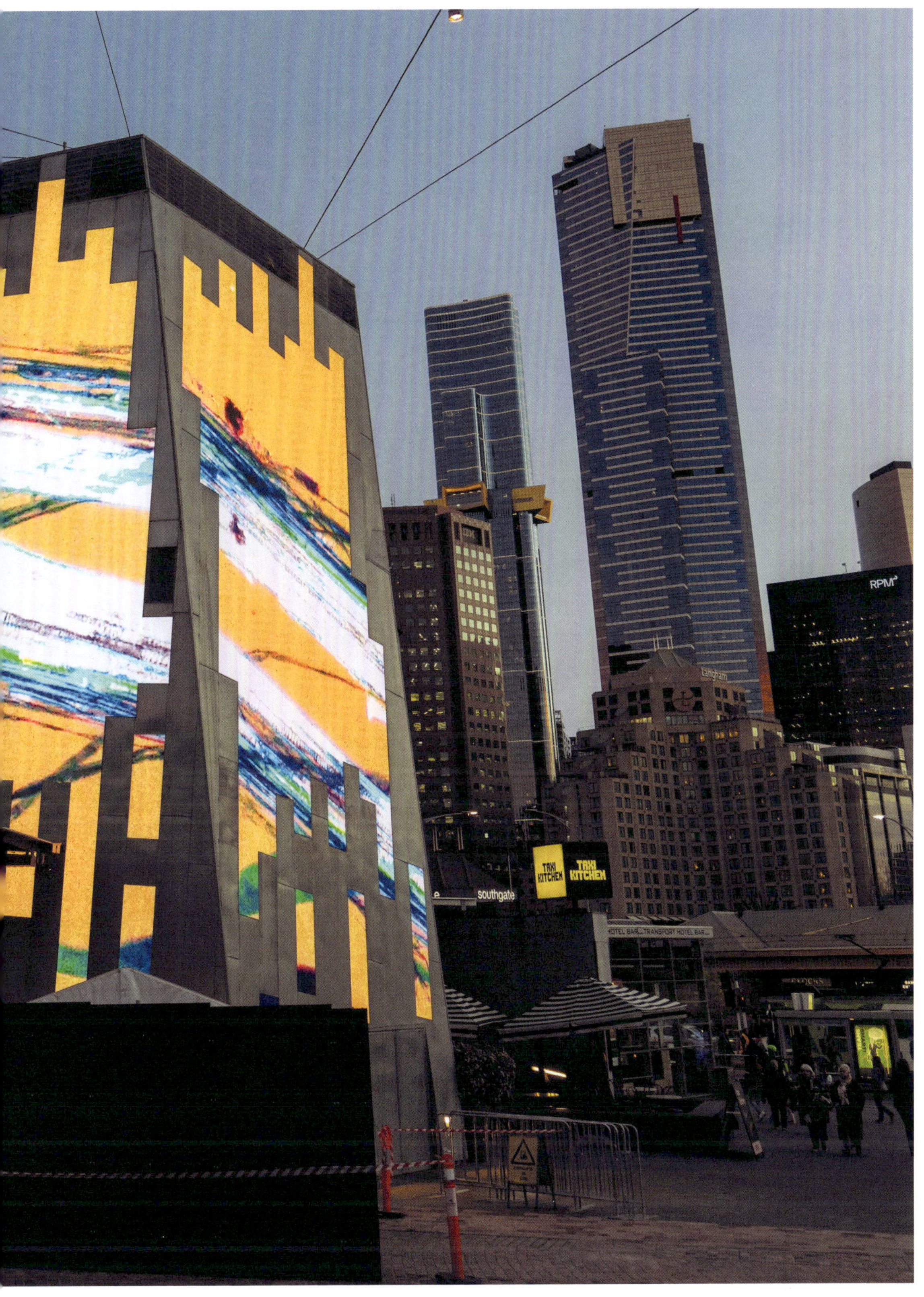
RPM
TAXI KITCHEN
TAXI KITCHEN
southgate

Artist Biographies

Maree Clarke

born 1961, Swan Hill,
lives and works in Naarm, Victoria

Maree Clarke is a Wamba Wamba, Mutti Mutti, and Boon Wurrung Yorta Yorta woman from North-West Victoria, and a multidisciplinary visual artist. Clarke is a pivotal figure in the reclamation of southeast Australian Aboriginal art practices, reviving elements of Aboriginal culture that were lost – or lying dormant – over the period of colonisation, as well as a leader in nurturing and promoting the diversity of contemporary southeast Aboriginal artists.

Clarke's continuing desire to affirm and reconnect with her cultural heritage has seen her revival of the traditions of possum skin cloak-making, body adornments and cultural objects in both traditional and contemporary materials. Additionally, her multimedia installations of photography including lenticular prints, 3D photographs and photographic holograms as well as painting, sculpture and video installation further explore the customary ceremonies, rituals and language of her ancestors.

Clarke has exhibited widely nationally and internationally in a range of contexts. In 2021, Clarke presented *Maree Clarke: Ancestral Memories*, a major solo retrospective exhibition at the National Gallery of Victoria, Melbourne, that celebrated three decades of her creative and cultural output. Clarke has also featured extensively in a range of biennials and group exhibitions including *Lorne Sculpture Biennale*, Lorne, 2022; *Tanarnthi: Festival of Aboriginal and Torres Strait Islander Art*, Art Gallery South Australia, Adelaide, 2022; *The National: New Australian Art,* Museum of Contemporary Art Australia, Sydney, 2021; and *Reversible Destiny*, Tokyo Photographic Museum, Tokyo, Tokyo, 2021.

In 2023, Clarke was awarded the Yalingwa Artist Fellowship in recognition of her significant contribution to creative practice in the Indigenous arts community in Victoria, and in 2022 received a nomination for Victorian Australian of the year. She has also participated in numerous national and international artist residencies on invitation, most recently at the Museum of Glass in Tacoma and at Pilchuck Glass School, Seattle USA.

Her work is held in major collecting institutions across Australia, as well as international collections including Monash University Art Collection, Prato Campus, Italy; Tokyo Photographic Museum, Tokyo; and Mount Holyoake College, Massachusetts, USA.

Maree Clarke is represented by Vivien Anderson Gallery, Melbourne, Australia.

Dean Cross

born 1986, Kamberri/Canberra
lives and works on Walbunja Country, New South Wales

Dean Cross is a paratactical artist interested in collisions of materials, ideas, and histories. Cross is motivated by the understanding that his practice sits within a continuum of the oldest living culture on Earth – and enacts First Nations sovereignty through expanded contemporary art methodologies. Through a cross-disciplinary practice that spans photography, video, installation, sculpture, painting, contemporary dance and choreography, Cross often confronts the legacies of modernism, rebalancing dominant cultural and social histories.

Cross has exhibited widely across Australia and beyond. Recent solo exhibitions include *To Be Clever, To Be Posh,* STATION, Melbourne, 2023; *Sometimes I Miss the Applause*, Heide Museum of Modern Art, Melbourne, 2022 and *Icarus, my Son*, Carriageworks, Sydney, 2021, and a two man show, *Things That are Real*, with acclaimed international artist Alvaro Barrington at Cement Fondu, 2023.

Recent group exhibitions include 2022 *Free/State: Adelaide Biennial of Australian Art:*, Art Gallery of South Australia, Adelaide, 2022; PHOTO2022: International Festival of Photography, Melbourne, 2022; *Primavera 2021: Young Australian Artists*, Museum of Contemporary Art Australia, Sydney, 2021; and *Eucalyptusdom*, The Museum of Applied Arts and Sciences, Sydney, 2021.

Cross was a finalist for the Wynne Prize, and the National Photographic Prize, MAMA Albury, in 2022, as well as the Ramsey Art Prize, Art Gallery of South Australia, Adelaide, 2021. Recent national and international artist residencies include Artist in Residence, The Clothing Store, Carriageworks, Sydney, 2019-2022; Indigenous Artist Exchange Canberra/Wellington, 2019, and 4A Centre for Contemporary Asian Art's Beijing Studio Residency, 2018.

Cross's work is held by major institutions including the Art Gallery of South Australia, the National Gallery of Victoria, the Heide Museum of Modern Art and The Museum of Applied Arts and Sciences, and in private collections in Australia, United States and France.

Dean Cross is represented by STATION Gallery, Melbourne.

Brad Darkson
born 1987, Kaurna yarta (Country), Tarntanya (Adelaide)
lives and works on Kaurna yarta, South Australia

Brad Darkson is a Narungga man and South Australian visual artist who works across various media including carving, sound, sculpture, multimedia installation, and painting. His creative and cultural practice is regularly focused on site specific works, and connections between contemporary and traditional cultural practice, language, and lore.

Conceptually Darkson's work is often informed by his First Nations and Anglo Australian heritage. His current research is focussed on traditional land management practices, bureaucracy, seaweed, and the neo-capitalist hellhole we're all forced to exist within.

From printing, casting, and carving to assemblages, sound, and performance, Darkson tends to be conceptually driven rather than materially focused. He first trained as a mechanic before turning his attention to artmaking and graduated with a Bachelor of Fine Art at the University of South Australia in 2015. This experience coupled with further research within a Master of Fine Art at the University of Tasmania shifted Darkson's focus to video, sculpture and sound installation and has proven a significant development in the spatial and experiential properties of his recent works.

Recently, Darkson has presented a major new commission for *Experimenta Lifeforms: International Triennial of Media Art*, touring nationally, 2021-23, and *VIETNAM — ONE IN, ALL IN*, which toured South Australia in 2019-2020. Solo exhibitions and events include *Make Yourself Comfortable,* Post Office Projects, Port Adelaide, 2022; *Tremendously very very very beautiful*, Guildhouse, Adelaide, 2021; UNCEDED LAND, Fine Print at the Art Gallery of South Australia, Adelaide, 2020; and *LOSS. GAIN. REVERB. DELAY*, Vitalstatistix for Tarnanthi: Festival of Aboriginal and Torres Strait Islander Contemporary Art, Port Adelaide, 2020. Selected group exhibitions include *The Return*, Hobart Convict Penitentiary, Dark Mofo, Museum of Old and New Art, Hobart 2018; and *old light (refraction),* Lot Fourteen, Adelaide 2020; *Hold Me, A//I* Adelaide International, Samstag Museum, Adelaide 2020; and *Neoteric,* Adelaide Railway Station, 2022.

Darkson currently sits on the board of The Australian Network for Art and Technology and the Guildhouse Artist Advisory Group. His work is held in the City of Adelaide Collection.

Matthew Harris
born 1991, Wangaratta
lives and works in Naarm/Melbourne, Victoria

Matthew Harris is a self-taught artist and current studio artist at Gertrude Contemporary of mixed European and Koorie descent. His multidicipinary contemporary art practice often debases dominant hierarchies through socially critical and conceptual painting and sculpture.

A queer sensibility and rhythmic seriality runs through his practice, with earlier works challenging conventions of taste and class, riffing on historical imagery with abject figuration in lurid colour palettes. More recently, Harris collides materials, traditional First Nations techniques and minimal abstraction in new ways.

Harris has exhibited widely in Australia as well as internationally. Select solo exhibitions include *Written on the Wind*, Milani Gallery Carpark, Brisbane, 2023; *Panopticon*, Conners Connors, Melbourne, 2022; *Spiritual Poverty*, Gertrude Glasshouse, Melbourne, 2022; *Doom*, Melbourne Art Fair, Melbourne, 2022; *Goo*, FUTURES, Melbourne, 2021; *The Simple Life*, Galerie Pompom, Sydney, 2021; *Hell*, Neon Parc, Melbourne, 2018.

His possum skin sculpture *Big Love,* 2021 was recently acquired by the National Gallery of Victoria, Melbourne and was presented in their major survey exhibition *Melbourne Now*, 2023.

Matthew Harris is represented by FUTURES, Melbourne.

James Howard
Born 1991, Naarm/Melbourne
lives and works on Boonwurrung Country, Victoria

James Howard is a Jaadwa song-man and composer with a contemporary music practice that investigates the soundscapes of Country and place. He approaches the process of composing as a way to reconnect with his Indigenous heritage, often layering personal and family narratives into long-form, improvised ambient works.

Howard utilises electronic instruments and production techniques, merging voice, analogue synthesizers, samples, and field recordings. His recent album, *Variations on Country*, 2021, uses an electronic sound palette to respond to intersections of Country, culture, politics, and identity.

In 2022, Howard collaborated with the Australian Dance Theatre to compose and record a soundtrack for the performance *The Third,* that has since been separately released as a new mini-album, *Music from 'The Third'*, 2022, exploring the body as archive, and the juncture of First Nations and Western knowledges. This collaboration led to a full-length score *SAVAGE,* also produced in collaboration with the Australian Dance Theatre, 2022.

Howard has worked collaboratively with a range of contemporary artists and arts organisations. He was commissioned by RISING Festival to develop the sound design for Dylan Mooney's new multimedia installation for the exhibition *Shadow Spirit*, 2023; and he was recently commissioned by The Australian Ballet to develop the soundtrack for the short film *ACT V*, 2021. Previously, Howard produced the score and soundtrack for the short film *mulunma — Inside, Within*, directed by Daniel Riley and commissioned by RISING Festival, in collaboration with Museums Victoria and YIRRAMBOI Festival, 2021. Howard was also a contributing artist for *Yulendji,* 2021, a public sound installation for YIRRAMBOI, commissioned by the Arts Centre Melbourne, 2021.

Howard holds a PhD in Indigenous Arts and Culture, having recently graduated from the Faculty of Fine Art and Music, University of Melbourne, in 2022 with his thesis *Composing Cultural Reclamation: Reconnecting to an Indigenous Cultural Heritage through a Music Practice.*

Hayley Millar Baker
born 1990, Naarm/Melbourne
lives and works on Boonwurrung and Wathaurong Country, Victoria

Hayley Millar Baker is a Gunditjmara and Djabwurrung woman, and multidisciplinary lens-based contemporary artist. Examining the role identities play in translating and conveying our experiences, Millar Baker works across photography, collage, and film to interrogate and make abstract the autobiographical narratives and themes relating to her own identity. Her oblique storytelling methods convey the passage of identity, culture, and memory as non-linear, and non-fixed.

Millar Baker's background in painting and photography has informed her most recent filmic works, *Nyctinasty* 2022, commissioned for *CEREMONY: 4th National Indigenous Art Triennial, National Gallery of Australia, Canberra,* and *The Umbra* 2023 *which* premiered in *Shadow Spirit* for *Rising Festival*, Melbourne, 2023.

In 2021-22, Millar Baker presented her first early career-survey exhibition *There we were all in one place* at UTS Gallery, Sydney, that brought together five pivotal bodies of work from Millar Baker's early career for the first time and has since toured nationally. Millar Baker has also exhibited as part of *Primavera 2018: Young Australian Artists* at the Museum of Contemporary Art, Sydney.

Millar Baker was awarded the John and Margaret Baker Memorial Fellowship for the *National Photography Prize* in 2020, the *Darebin Art Prize*, 2019, and *The Churchie National Emerging Art Prize* Special Commendation Award, 2017. Millar Baker has been a finalist in several prestigious national art prizes including; *Ramsay Art Prize*, 2019 and 2021, *Bowness Photography Prize*, 2021, *John Fries Award*, 2019, and international prizes including Italy's *Arte Laguna Prize*, Arsenale Nord, 2023; Hong Kong's *Sovereign Asian Art Prize*, 2021; and United Arab Emirates' *Vantage Point Sharjah 9*, 2021.

Millar Baker has been awarded several residencies, most recently the *Artist-in-residence* at Monash University Prato, Italy, 2022, and has featured in a range of festival-based exhibition projects including *PHOTO2021: International Festival of Photography*, 2021, *TELL: Contemporary Indigenous Photography,* International Ballarat Foto Biennale, 2017, and *Tarnanthi: Festival of Aboriginal and Torres Strait Islander Contemporary Art*, 2017.

Hayley Millar Baker is represented by Vivien Anderson Gallery, Melbourne, Australia.

Jazz Money
born 1992, Cammeraygal Country/Sydney
lives and works on Gadigal Country, New South Wales

Jazz Money is a Wiradjuri poet and artist whose creative and cultural practice encompasses installation, performance, film, and text-based works. Across these mediums Money's practice is centred around questions of narrative and legacy: place memory, First Nations memory, colonial memory and the stories that we tell to construct national and personal identity.

Their writing has been widely published and performed nationally and internationally, and performed on stages around the world, including TEDxSydney, Australia; Edinburgh International Book Festival, Scotland; Sydney Opera House, Australia; Literature Live! Mumbai, India; Performance Space New York, United States; Auckland Writers Festival, New Zealand; PEN International, online; among other arts and literary festivals.

Jazz's first poetry collection, the best-selling *how to make a basket,* 2021, published by University of Queensland Press, was the winner of the David Unaipon Award in 2020. Money was awarded the Australia Council for the Arts' prestigious Dreaming Award in 2022.

Money has presented work in a range of national exhibitions including *With Textual Consent*, La Trobe Art Institute, 2023; *How I See It*, ACMI, 2022; *Primavera 2022: Young Australian Artists,* Museum of Contemporary Art Australia, 2022; *Eucalyptusdom*, Museum of Applied Arts and Science, Sydney, 2021, and *Fremantle Biennale: Crossings*, for *Fremantle Biennale,* 2021. Money's major feature film *WINHANGANHA,* 2023, commissioned by the National Film and Sound Archive, will premiere at the British Film Institute in London before an international and national tour.

Money's work is held in major national collecting institutions Artbank, Australia; ACMI, Melbourne; La Trobe University, Melbourne; and University of Sydney Libraries, Sydney.

Money is a Clothing Store resident artist at Carriageworks in Sydney, 2023.

Mandy Quadrio
born 1959, Naarm/Melbourne
lives and works in Meanjin/Brisbane

Mandy Quadrio is a Trawlwoolway and Laremairemener Tasmanian Aboriginal artist working with sculpture and installation. Her creative and cultural practice works to unfix racist categorisations, historic denials, and the imposed invisibility in relation to Tasmanian Aboriginal people.

Through explorations with materiality, Quadrio extends her investigations into uncovering the hidden denials in Trouwunnan/Tasmanian history. To counteract ongoing myths and myth-conceptions about Palawa extinction, she engages historic and contemporary cultural objects and materials such as bull kelp, natural fibres and ochres, which she brings into conversation with industrially manufactured materials such as abrasive steel wool and steel wire-mesh to make up her 'cultural toolkit'. The harsh metallic fibres that she manipulates and transforms reference the forced indentured domestic labours of her forebears and the intentional, violent attempts to 'scrub out' the reality of ongoing Palawa existence. Through creative explorations Quadrio teases out the cultural and colonial associations of these materials to create new memories and histories for the nation.

Quadrio has exhibited widely both nationally and internationally. Upcoming and recent exhibitions include *Objects of Culture and Science,* Tasmania and Sweden, 2023; *Past, present, future,* Cairns Courthouse for Cairns Indigenous Art Fair, *2023*; *Terra Incognita: Inclusiveness is a good way,* San Teonisto Church, Treviso, Italy, 2022; *Beyond Misty Histories*, MONA FOMA, Hobart Town Hall Underground, 2022; *Water Rites,* Tarnanthi Festival of Aboriginal and Torres Strait Islander Contemporary Art, 2021. Quadrio presented an ambitious new commission *Whose time are we on?* for *Slow Moving Waters: TarraWarra Biennial,* 2021, Healesville, Victoria.

Quadrio has also been awarded and participated in a number of significant international artist residencies such as Konstepidemin Artist in Residence, Gothenburg, Sweden, 2023; First Nations Artists Cultural Exchange, Taiwan; Australia Council Delegation: Venice Biennale, Venice, Italy, 2022; and Australia Council Delegation: *rīvus Sydney Biennale*, Sydney, 2022. Her work has been acquired by the Queen Victoria Museum and Art Gallery, Launceston, and St Andrew's War Memorial Hospital, Brisbane.

Cassie Sullivan
born 1985, nipaluna/Hobart
lives and works on melukerdee Country, Tasmania

Cassie Sullivan is a palawa woman with a responsive, intimate, and experimental contemporary art practice that crosses disciplines of moving image, photography, writing, sound, installation, and printmaking. Sullivan works with a deeply considered process-driven practice that prioritises a sensory engagement with Country.

Within her creative and cultural practice, Sullivan uses writing to process and understand the way life moves around her; working to constantly question what can be imbued through materiality to give voice to complex identities.

Through a current research focus on exploring themes of intergenerational experience and trauma that reside in bodily memory, Sullivan investigates the ways in which knowledge from her Indigenous lineage has been both carried and lost within her identity and the body.

Sullivan's inaugural solo exhibition *Namesake*, 2017 was presented at Salamanca Arts Centre in Hobart. Since then, she has participated in group exhibitions including Int*erfacial Intimacies,* Plimsoll Gallery, 2023; *Down In The River*, Contemporary Art Tasmania, 2022; *Taking Up Space*, Schoolhouse Gallery, 2022; *Curing*, Kelly's Garden, Salamanca Arts Centre and The Barracks, New Norfolk, 2021; *The Pink Palace: From Isolation*, Schmørgåsbaag, Hobart, 2021 and *Scarring*, Hobart, 2022.

She has been shortlisted for the prestigious Women's Art Prize, 2021, Tasmania; the Moran Contemporary Photographic Prize, 2019; the Australian Institute of Professional Photography and The International Loupe Awards, 2011-2013.

Sullivan holds a Bachelor of Fine Arts with Honours, University of Tasmania, 2021, and a Diploma of Photoimaging, RMIT University, Victoria, 2011.

this mob
this mob is a blak arts collective based on Boonwurrung and Wurundjeri Country in Naarm/ Melbourne with members' ancestral connections in Victoria and across the country. Through their collaborative and relational process, this mob centre and prioritise Aboriginal and Torres Strait Islander people to create spaces to come together and unite emerging blak artists. By centring blakness, this mob carve out space for new ways for blak creative and cultural practice to exist and thrive in the art world that does not cater to whiteness.

As a collective, this mob come together on a regular basis at their artist studio in Collingwood Yards to take advantage of the rareness of having physical space to occupy. When together in the studio, their time is devoted to creating new artworks, sharing their individual practices and current projects with one another, and connecting with invited guests. Their shared studio provides the time and space for listening and yarning, and for rest; to be together without external pressure to produce or present.

this mob regularly facilitate community-centred knowledge sharing and skills-based workshops in life drawing, emu feather adornment making, collage, makeup, printmaking and more. Recent collective exhibitions include *Collective Movements,* Monash University of Modern Art, Melbourne, 2022; *Because of Her, We Can: HEAL,* Schoolhouse Studios, Melbourne, 2018; and *Yelmo Garang,* Footscray Community Arts Centre, Melbourne, 2017.

this mob members include:

Moorina Bonini
born 1996, Wurundjeri Country
lives and works on Wurundjeri Country, Victoria

Moorina Bonini is a proud descendant of the Yorta Yorta Dhulunyagen family clan of Ulupna and the Yorta Yorta, Wurundjeri and Wiradjuri Briggs/McCrae family. Her creative and cultural practice disrupts and critiques the Eurocentric foundations that centralise Indigenous categorisation within western institutions.

Kate ten Buuren
born 1994, Wurundjeri Country
lives and works on Kulin Country, Victoria

Kate ten Buuren is a Taungurung curator, artist and writer working on Kulin Country. Ten Buuren's cross-disciplinary practice investigates collective and collaborative ways of working, with her interest in contemporary visual art, film and oral traditions is grounded in self-determination and self-representation.

Maya Hodge
born 1998, Wurundjeri Country
lives and works on Wurundjeri Country, Victoria

Maya Hodge is a proud Lardil and Yangkaal emerging writer and curator. Her multidisciplinary practice explores the power of disrupting colonial narratives through writing, curatorial and musical project-based work dedicated to uplifting First Nations autonomy and storytelling.

Jenna Rain Warwick
born 1997, Kuku Yalanji Country
lives and works on Wurundjeri Country, Victoria

Jenna Rain Warwick is an artist, curator and published writer born in Mossman, Queensland. A proud Luritja Woman, her practice centres her love for film and television. She has curated film programs and screenings, and has a desire to reinvigorate film criticism in so called 'Australia'.

Jenna Lee
born 1992, Ngunnawal Country
lives and works on Wurundjeri Country, Victoria

Jenna Lee is a Gulumerridjin (Larrakia), Wardaman and KarraJarri Saltwater woman with mixed Japanese, Chinese, Filipino and Anglo-Australian ancestry. Using art to explore and celebrate her many overlapping identities, Lee works across sculpture, installation, and body adornment.

Contributor Biographies

Tina Baum
lives and works in Kamberri (Australian Capital Territory)

Tina Baum, Gulumirrgin-Larrakia/Wardaman/Karajarri peoples, has over 30 years working in Australian Museums and Galleries. She is a writer and the Curator of Aboriginal and Torres Strait Islander Art at the National Gallery of Australia since 2005. She curated the *Defying Empire: 3rd National Indigenous Art Triennial*, 2017, the *Ever Present: First Peoples Art of Australia*, 2021-23 national and international touring exhibition and the *Emerging Elders* exhibition, 2009.

Baum is a recipient of the Australia Council for the Arts 2022-23 International Curators Program Asia Pacific Triennial x TarraWarra Biennial, the 2021-22 Art Monthly Australasia, Indigenous Voices Program (writing) as a mentor, the Australia Council for the Arts, Arts Leaders Program, 2020-22, and the inaugural British Council Accelerate Programme to the UK, 2009. She is a mentor to alumni, presenter and organiser of the NGA and Wesfarmers Indigenous Arts Leadership and Fellowship Programs since 2010.

She is passionate about embedding Indigenous voices, perspectives and truth telling and Indigenising best practice methodologies within Museum and Galleries throughout Australia and internationally by reasserting Indigenous traditional language, cultural authority and agency.

Natalie Harkin
lives and works in Kaurna Yarta (South Australia)

Natalie Harkin is a Narungga poet and academic living on Kaurna Yarta, South Australia, and currently a Research Fellow at Flinders University. She engages archival-poetic methods to document community Memory Stories, decolonise state archives, and she is a member of South Australia's inaugural State Records/State Library of South Australia's Aboriginal Reference Group. Her research centres on Aboriginal women's domestic service and labour histories, and Indigenous Living-Legacy/Memory Story archiving innovations for our time. Her words have been installed and projected in mixed-media exhibitions, including creative-arts research collaboration with *Unbound Collective*. She is widely published, and her manuscripts include *Dirty Words*, Cordite Books, 2015, *Archival-poetics*, Vagabond Press, 2019, and *APRON-SORROW / SOVEREIGN-TEA,* Wakefield Press, in-press, 2021.

Curator Biography

Jessica Clark
born nipaluna/Hobart, lutruwita/trouwerner (Tasmania)
lives and works on Wurundjeri Country

Jessica Clark is a proud palawa/pallawah woman with English, Irish, Turkish, and French ancestry. She is a curator of contemporary art living and working on Wurundjeri Country in Naarm/Melbourne. Clark currently holds the position of Yalingwa Curator at the Australian Centre for Contemporary Art, 2022-24. Her background in art history and art education has informed the development of an independent curatorial practice that is guided by conversation and collaboration, and grounded in an understanding of the interrelationship between life, materiality, and place. Recent independent and collaborative exhibition projects include *breathing space*, and *one (&) another*, Margaret Lawrence Gallery, Naarm, 2021 and 2020; *In and of this place*, Benalla Art Gallery Online, 2021, and *Experimenta Life Forms: International Triennial of Media Art* national touring exhibition, 2021-2023. Clark is a participant in the *International Curators* Program: Asia Pacific Triennial x TarraWarra Biennial, 2021-2023 and alumni of PIAD: First Nations Colloquium, South Africa, 2019, Darwin Aboriginal Art Fair Cultural Keepers Program, 2017-2020, Wesfarmers Indigenous Arts Leadership Program, 2018, Signature Works: Innovation Lab, 2018, and the First Nations Curators Program for the Venice Biennale, 2017. She is a recent graduate of the Victorian College of the Arts, University of Melbourne, having completed a curatorial practice-led PhD that investigated intercultural curatorial models for contemporary Australian art.

Curator Acknowledgements

Between Waves was developed, and is presented on the unceded lands of the Wurundjeri and Boonwurrung peoples of the south-eastern Kulin Nation – the lands I now call home in Naarm/ Melbourne. I respectfully acknowledge that art and culture has been thriving here, and across the continent now called Australia since time immemorial, and I pay my deepest respect to Elders past, present and future.

I am a proud palawa/pallawah woman with English, Irish, Turkish, and French ancestry, born in nipaluna/ Hobart, and as such, I acknowledge my ancestors, Elders, Country, and community at home, and the many places I have lived and worked. I would particularly like to acknowledge the Kulin Nation and Kaurna Country.

My heartfelt thanks to the *Between Waves* artists, for our yarns, for the opportunity to work together, and present their incredible new work in this exhibition. Equally, I extend sincere thanks to commissioned writers Tina Baum and Nat Harkin for their thoughtful and considered contributions to the exhibition catalogue. I respectfully acknowledge the artists and writers' ancestors, cultural knowledges, and the wide-ranging places they call home. I give my warmest gratitude to the Yalingwa Directions Circle: Aunty Joy Murphy Wandin AO (chair), Kylie Belling, Belinda Briggs, Hetti Perkins, Stacie Piper and Hannah Presley for their encouragement and support through exhibition development. I would also like to acknowledge the First Peoples team at Creative Victoria and the Yalingwa Visual Arts Initiative for this curatorial opportunity, as well as the support of TarraWarra Museum of Art and Victoria Lynn, Director.

An exhibition of this scope would not have been possible without the ongoing support of my incredible colleagues at the Australian Centre for Contemporary Art (ACCA). In particular, I would like to acknowledge and thank Director Max Delany for his ongoing support, as well as curatorial colleagues Shelley McSpedden and Elyse Goldfinch, the executive team Laura De Neefe and Claire Richardson, operations manager, Margaret Stern, development team Grace Fraraccio and Kathryne Honey, publicist Katrina Hall, and previous ACCA curator Miriam Kelly. I extend my thanks to ACCA's amazing exhibition manager Samantha Vawdrey, and her dedicated install team for bringing *Between Waves* into being, as well as technical advisors Charlie Farmer and Joon Youn, and the entire extended team at ACCA.

I would equally like to thank the various artists' collaborators and gallerists, among other friends, colleagues and supporters, who have contributed to so many aspects of the exhibition. I also acknowledge with appreciation Sarah Tutton, Mary Parker and Kate ten Buuren for their support of Maree Clarke's projection at Federation Square, and Julie Kantor and Wesley Enoch for their contribution to the Curatorial Symposium program.

Finally, all my love to my family incredible family, and friends who are family, for their guidance, care, and support, in particular my parents Between Meade and Rodney Clark. I would also like to acknowledge my mentors Maree Clarke, Lee-Ann Tjunypa Buckskin, Tina Baum, Dr David Sequeira, and Natalie King OAM.

Artists' Acknowledgements

Maree Clarke would like to thank Dorian Farr from Shadowlab for the beautiful multimedia work on my microscopic river reeds for the Federation Square big screen; Vivien Anderson and Amy Boyd for their continued support of my practice and Jess Clark for inviting me to be part of *Between Waves,* which gave me the opportunity to work with Chris and Laura in the Histology department at the University of Melbourne to make this new work.

Brad Darkson would like to Chloe and Guthrie for, 'supporting me throughout my arts practice. I miss you every day I'm at the studio!'

James Howard would like to thank Alanna Solole, Transurban Maintenance Manager, Victoria; Lee Harrower, Transurban Maintenance Closure Supervisor; Rita Kourellas, Transurban Operations Administration, Road Operations and Melbourne Electronic Sound Studio.

Jazz Money would like to thank Jessica Clark and the wider ACCA team for making this work possible. And always Jenn.

Cassie Sullivan would like to thank John Robinson from Moving Creature Studio, Tasmania as well as staff from the Victorian College of the Arts, University of Melbourne including Lisa Radford, Mark Friedlander and Simone Slee.

Project Team

Curator
Jessica Clark

Exhibition Manager
Samantha Vawdrey

Editor
Jessica Clark

Copyeditor and Editorial Production
Elyse Goldfinch

Installation Team
Marty de Jesus
Edward de Souza
Charlie Farmer
Kubota Fumikazu
Casey Jeffery
Jacob Raupach
Brian Scales
Nicholas Smith

Publication Designer
Matt Hinkley

Photography
Andrew Curtis

Digital Wing Production
Rowan McNaught

Print
Adams Print

Dulux Paint Colours
Jodhpurs yellow

ACCA Board

John Denton, Chair
Fayen d'Evie
Alana Kushnir
Sarah Lynn Rees
Andrew Taylor
Gordon Thomson
Dr Terry Wu

ACCA Staff

Max Delany
Artistic Director & CEO

Claire Richardson
Executive Director

Laura De Neefe
Director, Development & Engagement

Shelley McSpedden
Senior Curator

Jessica Clark
Curator

Elyse Goldfinch
Curator, Public Programs & Publications

Samantha Vawdrey
Exhibitions Manager

Anita King
Project Manager, ACCA Beyond Walls

Margaret Stern
Operations Manager

Hana Vasak
Visitor Experience & Events Manager

Grace Fraraccio
Development & Digital Content Coordinator

Kathryne Honey
Development & Marketing Coordinator

Felicia Pinchen-Hogg
Education Manager (parental leave)

Edwina Hill
Acting Education Manager

Minna Lappalainen
Education & Access Coordinator

Lauren Simmonds
Artist Educator

Maggie Lu
Accounts Coordinator

Matt Hinkley
Designer

Katrina Hall
Publicist

Visitor Experience Coordinators
Arini Byng
Monique Chiari
Emily Hubbard
Ponie Curtis
Ruth Cummins

Visitor Experience Team
Nicholas Anderson
Beatrice Gabriel
Danielle Goder
Suzannah Griffith
Dhariz Manalo
Jacinta Maude
Leah Nathan
Luka Rhoderick

Volunteers
Beatriz Airah Yu
Jasmine Babayan
Alec Bolwell
Jess Chow
Jessica Ebeyer
Arty Foulkes
Harper Hamilton-Grutzner
Gala Hazel
Enya Hu
Alissa Lad
Maria McGowan Grace
Chanthicha Meekun-iam
Declan Monaghan
Julie Monaghan
Matilda Mourant
Amy Naylor
Lauren Nevard
Kirra Niner
Elyse O'Neill
Shaarn Pateman
Phillip Patterson
China Paul
Meyrick Payne
Mikayla Poon
Yongpin Ren
Moksha Richards
Mythra Sage
Katinka Samuel
Daniel Song
CJ Starc
Sylva Storm
Scarlet Sykes
Hesterman
Josh V.E.
Chloe Vella
Dominique Viggiani
Indiana Wells
Sinéad Wheeler
Anna Xiang

ACCA Donors

Visionary
The Macfarlane Fund
J. Andrew Cook
& Prof. Wendy Brown
Vivien & Graham
Knowles

Champion
Michael & Janet Buxton
John Denton
& Susan Cohn
Bruce Parncutt AO
Megan Ponsford
& Noel Fermanis
Michael Schwarz
& David Clouston
Dr Terry Wu
& Dr Melinda Tee
Prescott Family
Foundation

Guardian
Lesley Alway & Paul
Hewison
Australia China Art
Foundation
Sam & Tania Brougham
Rosemary Forbes
& Ian Hocking
Judith & Leon Gorr
Marita & James Lillie
Emeritus Professor
Margaret Plant
Frank Pollio
Porsche Cars Australia
Pty Ltd
Craig Semple
Chris & Cheryl Thomas
Marita Onn & John Tuck
Rosemary Walls

Patron
Anthony & Michele
Boscia
Paul & Samantha Cross
Georgia Dacakis
Andy Dinan
& Mario Lo Giudice
Peter & Leila Doyle
Sophie Gannon
Rachel Griffiths
& Andrew Taylor
Lou & Will McIntyre
Mark Nelson
Jan van Schaik
Sarah & Ted Watts
Anonymous (2)

Friend
Paul Auckett
Lyn & Rob Backwell
Professor Andrew
Benjamin
Beth Brown
Bird de la Coeur
Architects
Ingrid Braun
Jon & Gabrielle Broome
Sue Dodd
Jane Hemstritch
Alana Kushnir
& Shaun Cartoon
Launch Housing
Elizabeth Leslie
Gene-Lyn Ngian
& Jeffrey Robinson
Drew Pettifer
Sue Rose & Alan Segal
Susan M Renouf
Jane Ryan
& Nick Kharsas
Naomi Ryan
Bernard Shafer
Steven Smith
STATION
Jennifer Strauss AM
Fiona Sweet
& Paul Newcombe
Irene Sutton
Noel & Jenny Turnbull
Lyn Williams AM
Anonymous (5)

Contemporary
Sally Browne AM
Elly Fink
Emily Floyd
Lesa-Belle Furhagen
Vida Maria Gaigalas
Nicholas Lolatgis
Angela Rutherford
& Vincenzo Giarrusso
Allan & Eva Rutman
Dr Nigel Simpson
Anonymous (3)

Enthusiast
Sandy & Damian
Abrahams
Julia Gardiner
John McNamara
Kenneth W Park
Raffaele Cotroneo
Anonymous (4)

Partners

Presenting Partner

Exhibition Partners

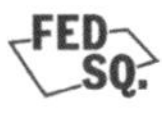

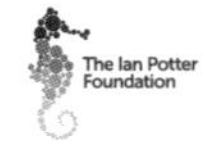

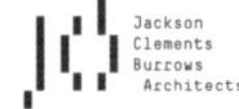

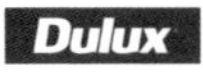

Curatorial Symposium Partner

Annamila

Exhibition Donor

Craig Semple

Media Partner

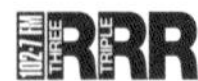

Touring Partners

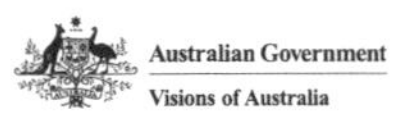

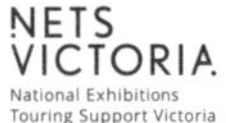

NETS Victoria Supporters

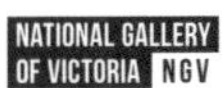

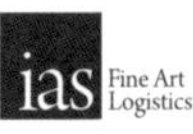

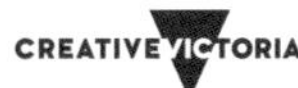

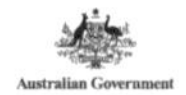

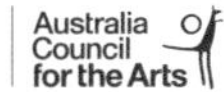

National Exhibitions Touring Support (NETS) Victoria is supported by the Victorian Government through Creative Victoria, by the Australian Government through the Australia Council, its arts funding and advisory body, and through the Visual Arts and Craft Strategy, an initiative of the Australian, State and Territory Governments. NETS Victoria also receives significant in-kind support from the National Gallery of Victoria.

ACCA Partners and Supporters

ACCA Government Partners

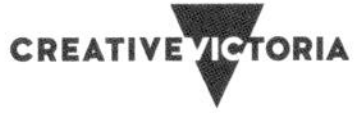

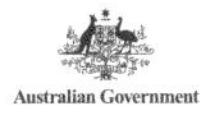

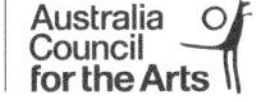

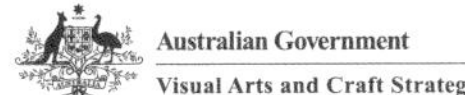

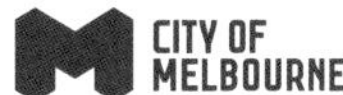

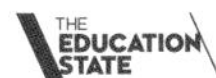

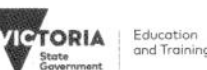

Network Partners

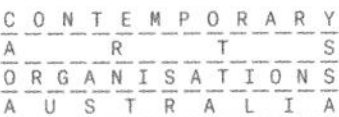

Partners

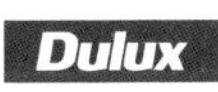

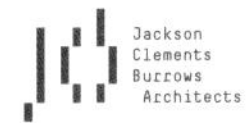

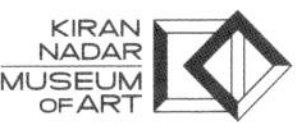

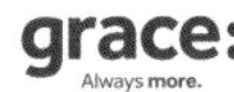

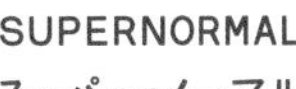

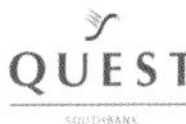

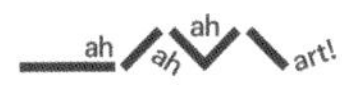

Media Partners

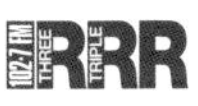

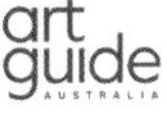

The Monthly
The Saturday Paper
7am

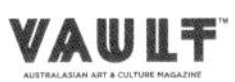

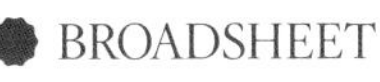

Event Partners

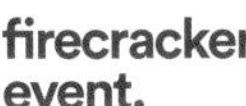

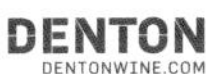

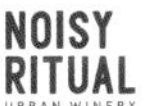

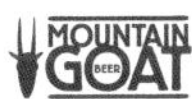

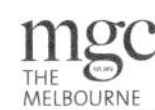

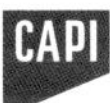

Trusts and Foundations

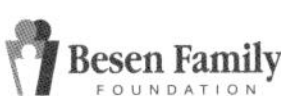

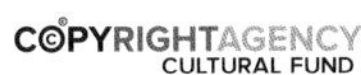

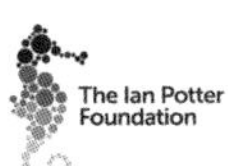

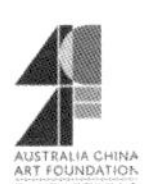

Supporters

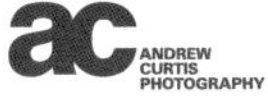

ACCA acknowledges the generous support of various government, philanthropic and corporate organisations that enable ACCA to continue to impact artists and audiences. In particular, we acknowledge the Australian Government through the Australia Council, its principal arts funding and advisory body; the Victorian Government through Creative Victoria; as well as the support of City of Melbourne.

Between Waves
Australian Centre
for Contemporary Art

1 July – 3 September 2023

Curator: Jessica Clark

Published 2023
© Australian Centre for
Contemporary Art,
artists and authors
ISBN: 978-0-6458328-1-5

The views and opinions
expressed in this publication
are those of the authors.
No material, whether
written or photographic,
may be reproduced without
permission of the artists,
authors and Australian
Centre for Contemporary Art.

Australian Centre for
Contemporary Art
111 Sturt Street
Southbank VIC 3006
Melbourne, Australia
acca.melbourne

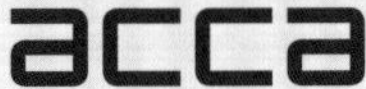

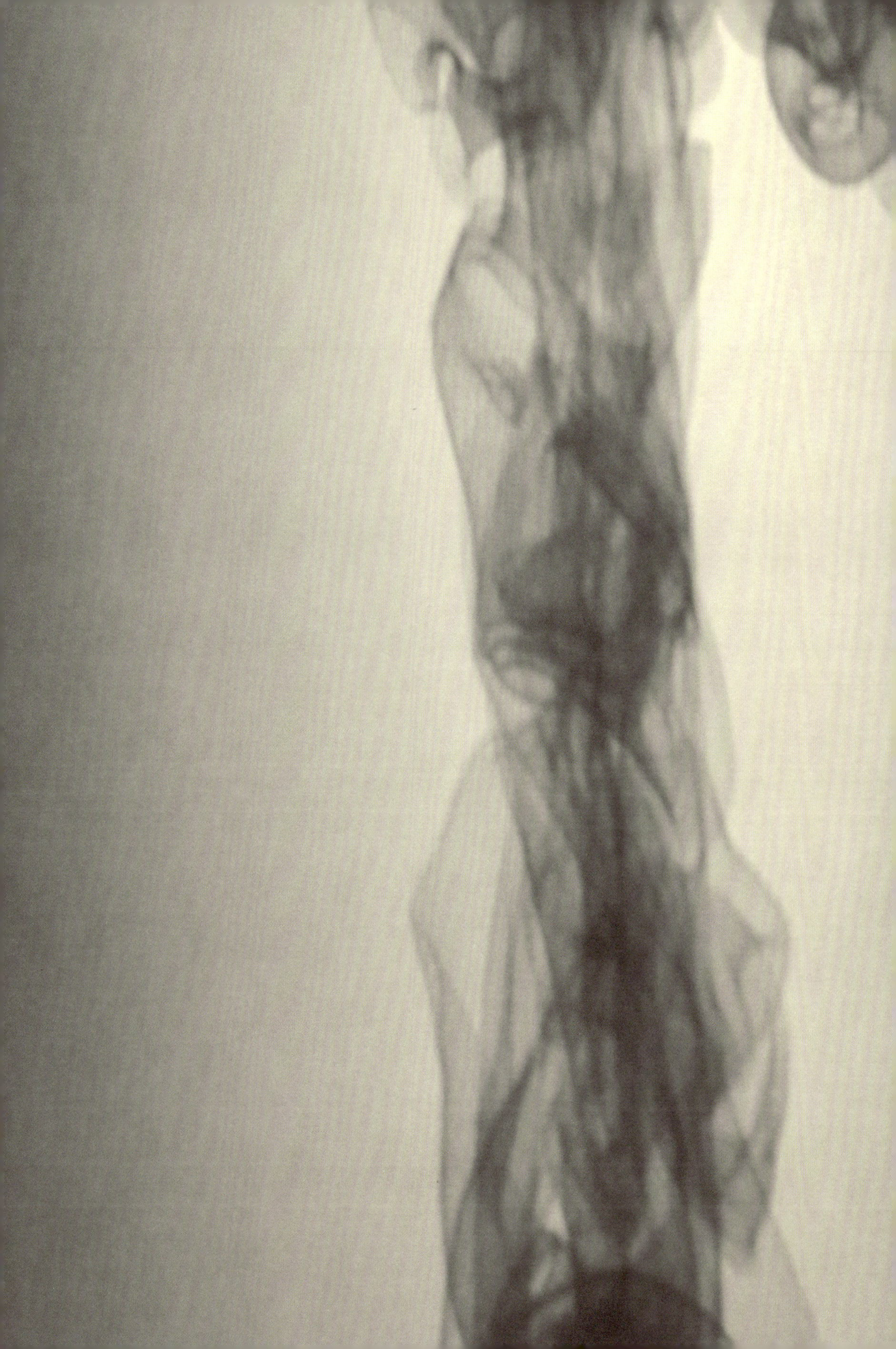

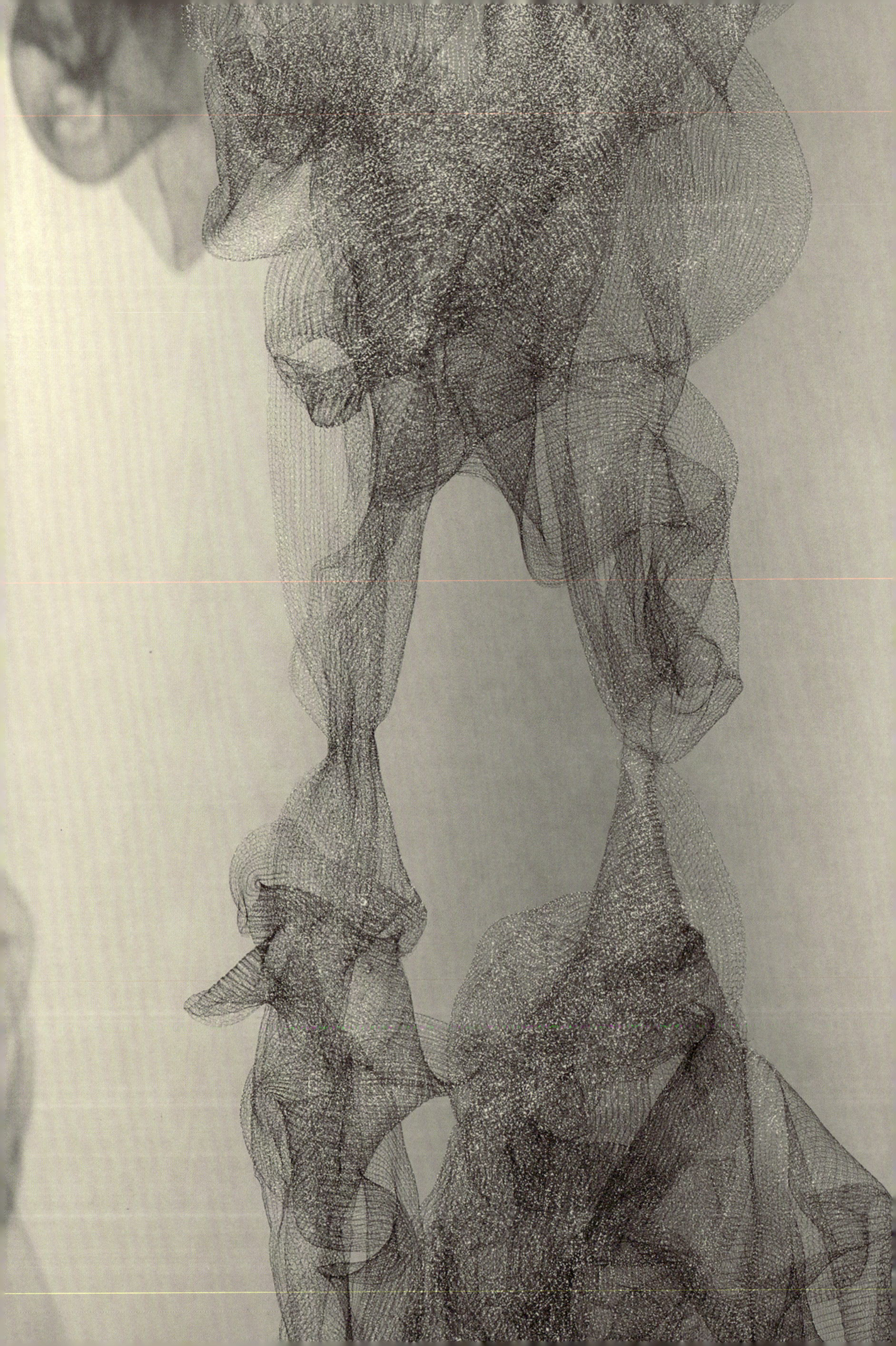